FORTY LESSONS TO 40

Wisdom for Navigating Through Life's Journey

LaShawn Spry

Copyright © LaShawn Spry | Forty Lessons to 40

Prepared by: Ebony Nicole Smith | www.EbonyNicoleSmith.com

All rights reserved. This book is protected by the copyright laws of the United States of America. No portion of this book may be stored electrically, transmitted, copied, reproduced or reprinted for commercial gain or profit without prior written permission from the author, LaShawn Spry. Permission request may be mailed to the address below. Only the use of short quotations or occasional page copying for personal or group study is allowed without written permission.

Send your request to *lashawn@lashawnspryencounter.com*.

All Scripture quoted/referenced from the King James Version of the Bible published by Barbour Publishing, Inc | ©2012 Barbour Publishing | www.barbourbooks.com

This book and other titles by LaShawn Spry can be found at: *www.lashawnspryencounter.com*

Printed in the U.S.A

ISBN 13- 978-0-692-18007-5

Book cover designed by Robert E. Spry | RES Ministries

Front and back cover photographed by: 2 Chix with a Camera, LLC | www.2chixwithacamera.com

Editor: CaTyra Polland | Chief Editor | www.pollandllc.com

First Edition: December 2018

DEDICATION

This book is dedicated to every woman committed to acquiring all the information that life has to offer. May you implement the lessons you learn and become the woman you were predestined to be.

.

CONTENTS

FORWARD 1

LESSON 1: 5

"Control What You Can and Surrender the Rest to God"

LESSON 2: 12

"Resilience is Your Super Power"

LESSON 3: 17

"Protect Your Energy"

LESSON 4: 21

"Anger is an Unproductive Emotion"

LESSON 5: 28

"Perfectionism is an Illusion"

LESSON 6: 34

"Confidence is Necessary for Success"

LESSON 7: 40

"Your Actions Are Your Responsibility"

LESSON 8: 45

"Peace is Priceless"

LESSON 9: 51

"Be You"

LESSON 10: 57

"Vulnerability is Necessary"

LESSON 11: 64

"You're Stronger Than You Think"

LESSON 12: 69

"Know Your True Identity"

LESSON 13: 75

"It's Never Too Late"

LESSON 14: 81

"We Are Forever Becoming"

LESSON 15: 87

"Your Vision Creates Your Reality"

LESSON 16: 92

"Shift Your Focus"

LESSON 17: 97

"It's Still Fly to be a Lady"

LESSON 18: 103

"The Why Factor"

LESSON 19: 108

"Love Your Future Self Enough"

LESSON 20: 113

"Truth Heals"

LESSON 21: 119

"You Train People How to Treat You"

LESSON 22: 125

"Not Everyone Can Handle All of You"

LESSON 23: 130

"An Apology Isn't Always Enough"

LESSON 24: 135

"True Friendship Takes Time"

LESSON 25: 140

"Cherish Life's Jewels; You're Only Gifted a Few"

LESSON 26: 145

"Let Your Light Shine"

LESSON 27: 150

"Remain Unbothered by the Opinions of People"

LESSON 28: 155

"Healed People, Heal People"

LESSON 29: 162

"Let Pride Die"

LESSON 30: 169

"There is a Process to Greatness"

LESSON 31: 177

"Extend the Grace and Mercy You Want to Receive"

LESSON 32: 183

"Love Is All You Need"

LESSON 33:	188

"Nothing Just Happens"

LESSON 34:	194

"Much Prayer, Much Power"

LESSON 35:	200

"God's Grace is Sufficient"

LESSON 36:	206

"Divine Connections Are Powerful"

LESSON 37:	212

"Forgiveness: The Gift that Keeps on Giving"

LESSON 38:	217

"Your Process Prepares You for Your Unique Purpose"

LESSON 39:	223

"The Gift of Gratitude"

LESSON 40:	229

"Take God at His Word"

ACKNOWLEDGMENTS	234
ABOUT THE AUTHOR	235

Forty Lessons to 40

FORWARD

I must say I am totally grateful for the opportunity to be asked to write the foreword for such an amazing book. Being afforded this chance is humbling and a privilege that I don't take lightly.

There aren't many opportunities in life when you are graced to meet the person of your dreams. God who is wise in His decision making, will tailor make the perfect individual just for you. I've been blessed beyond what I could ever imagine to be married to LaShawn Davis-Spry, who I always refer to as my "Grace Gift" from God. The moment she showed up in my life I knew we would be able to build a strong future together. Her passion, commitment, love and endurance are just a few qualities of her character. I take joy in knowing that she was made just for me!

One of the things I admire most about my wife is her desire to share her story with anyone that will listen. Her transparency about the things she endured from past relationships and life decisions, cannot be ignored. Her story is a mirror of what a survivor looks like. Countless nights we would sit up talking and she would share vivid descriptions of some of the things that she endured. I knew in those moments if she shared her testimony with the masses, their lives would be changed forever.

Life is a journey that often leads to pain, pressurized moments and problems that seem irreversible. This thing called life will lead us through valleys, deserts, seasons of desolation, pitfalls and dark caves. At times it feels like this is all life has to offer. From my own experience frustration will set in as well as fatigue and hopelessness. Out of desperation you do all you can to get yourself out of the predicament that so grips your life. At times, the search for answers seems to lead you down a path of confusion and internal emptiness. But, I have good news for you my friend, the search is over. You have literally found a book that holds the solution to your plaguing problems. If this book were written in the early stages of my life, I'm sure I could've avoided most of the challenges that I encountered. The content revealed on the pages of this book will revolutionize your life.

"Forty Lesson to 40" is a book that gives hope to those

who think hope can't be restored. It is a resource that gives great insight to relational issues that one maybe be facing. It is also a wisdom guide on how to bounce back from life altering situations. One of the best qualities about this book is, it sheds light on how to recover from domestic and mental abuse. There are so many great pointers that *"Forty Lessons to 40"* has to offer. It's a hub that houses diverse scenarios coupled with precise wisdom nuggets to help the reader handle the different issues that life presents.

LaShawn's candid depiction of her own personal experiences will help you avoid those same occurrences that can cause you years of pain and anguish. In addition, it teaches you how to manage and recover when life seems unfair. I challenge you to read this book from cover to cover and apply the principles that are found in each lesson. Take out a pencil and write down key points that literally speak to where you are NOW! Rehearse them daily until you start to see a difference in your life. Listen, change can only happen when we discipline ourselves and apply the tools necessary to produce results. You may find yourself going through some of the same things that are mentioned on these pages, but I promise you this book will be your guide on how to live beyond where you are right now. Make the commitment not to put this book down until the lessons are learned, and you see your life has improved.

Pastor Robert E. Spry II
First Baptist Church of Collier City

LESSON 1:

"Control What You Can and Surrender the Rest to God"

"You may not control all the events that happen to you, but you can decide not to be reduced by them." (Maya Angelou)

Planning is something that has always come second nature to me. As early as elementary school I can remember being very well organized. As soon as I got home from school I would complete my homework without being told and study for tests if necessary. I would then get my things together, straighten up my room and pick out my clothes for the next day. Even as early as 4 and 5 I hated when things occurred outside of my routine. Any deviations from my regular plans would throw me completely off. That same truth followed me into adulthood.

As a young wife and mother of two, I would strategically plan every day of my life. From what my children would eat, what they would wear to school, and what I would wear to work. I planned what time I would leave the house and get them to school and the estimated time I would need to get from there to work. I planned the purchase of a brand-new home, new car, a pickup truck and even the type of dog I would have. I planned the décor in our home, pink room for her and blue for him, where my children would attend school and even what college they would go to and the career paths they would take. I had

EVERYTHING planned out...or so I thought.

What I did not plan for was the mental and physical abuse that I would feel the effects of for many years to come. I didn't plan for infidelity, on both parts. Divorce after ten years of marriage and the loss of everything I worked so hard to obtain wasn't in my well laid out plan either. I wasn't ready for a custody battle so grueling that not only cost me every dime I had, but literally almost cost me my life! I wasn't equipped to handle the pressure that came when life was out of my control.

After the divorce was final, I lost my identity. Partying had become my middle name, sex was my drug of choice and alcohol my best friend. I was a preacher's kid raised as Christian, but as an adult I didn't have a strong personal relationship with God. I knew even as a child that there was a call on my life (for those that don't know, that just means God had something special for me to do) but I had strayed so far away from my church roots, that I didn't know how to get back nor did I have a desire at the time. In my mind it was God that put me in this position anyway, right?! That's how I felt, and that method of thinking drove me further and further away from the one sure hope that I had left.

One night while sitting on the floor in my bedroom, consumed by all that I was going through, I broke down. I wished it would all just end; the pain, the anger, the heartache and loneliness. I was physically drained, emotionally defeated and my heart was completely broken. This was not unlike many other nights I suffered through, but that night I was prepared to end it. I owned a 9mml Glock gifted to me by my ex-husband for my 25th birthday. (oh, the irony). I kept the gun at the top of the closet in a locked box, with an additional lock on the actual gun itself. As I lie on the floor, eyes closed shut and head feeling like it would explode, I envisioned myself going to get the gun. I could clearly see myself walk slowly into the closet and reach up for the black box. I sat down on the floor with the box in my lap. I attempted to open it and this time the box was NOT locked. I picked up my gun, both the trigger lock and safety were off. It almost felt as if something wanted me to take my life and not have a moment to think twice. I sat there looking down at the gun in my hands. I thought of all the times I'd been taught that suicide was a sin but couldn't think of one time that I'd been taught what to do with all the pain I was experiencing. Not one time was I prepared to handle the pressures of not being in complete control. I stared down at the gun in my hands.

Suddenly, I jumped up, grabbing my chest and gasping for air. I was TERRIFIED! It felt as if someone was holding my head under water and had finally decided to let me go. I took a few deep breaths to get my breathing under control. I looked around and realized I never moved from that cold spot on the floor of my bedroom. I'd cried so much until I fell asleep and the plans I'd made for myself played out in a dream. For the first time in my adult life, I cried out to God for help. All I could get out was, "God please help me. Please, I can't do this, help me." I heard a voice as if the person were in the room with me saying, "I'm here, give it to me. You don't have to do this by yourself. I love you. Give it to Me." I cried until eventually I fell asleep again.

That night was the beginning of a very long process that, for me, continues to this day; the art of surrender. While there is nothing wrong with having a plan in place and exercising your organizational skills, it is a whole different beast to be rocked and rattled when life happens. A different type of struggle is presented when your peace and joy are interrupted by the things that happen or don't happen outside of your realm of control. God is the only one that knows all things, is everywhere and has all power. He is the only one that controls what has been, currently is and what shall be. Surrendering every care, every worry, concern, circumstance and decision to God is the very best gift you can give yourself. The Word says, "Cast all your cares on Him because He cares for you." This doesn't give you control, but directly connects you to the One with ALL control!!

Lesson Principles:

1. While preparation and organization are great skills to have, trust in God *is* your number one priority.

2. Know that God is always working behind the scenes on your behalf.

3. There is nothing that will ever happen concerning you that God is not aware of.

Let's Pray:

Father, in the name of Jesus, the Bible declares in Psalms 55:22, "Cast your cares on the Lord and He will sustain you; He will never let the righteous fall." Lord, there are times when things happen outside of my control and it feels like I'm not going to make it. Bring Your Word back to my remembrance to give You all my worries and cares, knowing that You will never let me fall. In Jesus' name. Amen.

LESSON 2:

"Resilience is Your Super Power"

"Resilience is all about being able to overcome the unexpected. Sustainability is about survival. The goal of resilience is to thrive." (Jamais Cascio)

Reflection is always a useful tool, especially during life's difficult seasons. It reminds us where we've come from and where we're headed. It shows what we have already endured and persevered through. Reflection exposes our weaknesses, while unveiling our strengths. It gives us a snapshot of those that were there for us and the ones that chose to leave. It can silence our doubts and strengthen our faith. It's something that I've committed to doing regularly. In doing so, I've realized the power I possess.

I must say over the last 20 years I have faced an amalgam of difficulties. I can recall the times I didn't think I would make it through. I remember the heartaches, heartbreaks and betrayals of trust that I felt I would never fully recover from. The hurt I'd caused others and had the hardest time forgiving myself for. I remember the moments I said to myself, "This time you've gone too far." Some of this was just life happening and other times it was my own irresponsible decision making. Nonetheless, when I look back over the years I can clearly see resilience at work within me.

At some point during each life altering event,

whether it was a divorce, car repossession, eviction, loss of a loved one or friend, I felt as if it were the end for me. One of the worst times of my life was losing custody of my children. I can clearly recall the way I felt when the mediator read aloud the decision to award primary custody of my children to their father. The breath literally left my body. Because of the depth of the blow, I thought I would never recover. Yet, every night that I lie down and every morning that I rose served as proof that I could make it; I WOULD make it! You see, while I was focused on the magnitude of the pain and degree of suffering I was experiencing, I couldn't see the truth. The truth of the matter is that I was still alive. The fact that I was still alive meant I still had a purpose greater than any pain I'd experienced. Every hurt that was behind me said I was equipped with the necessary tools to withstand another. The unexpected circumstances made me bend, but I would not break. Resilience says I will not only survive, I will thrive.

Difficulties, challenges and setbacks are an unavoidable part of life. Don't fret! These periods of time will build your endurance muscles. They expose and train your strength and teach you that you can persevere. Once you learn to tap into your inner source of strength, you'll never fear falling again. Even when you are down, you know that you have everything you need to rise to the top again because you my dear are RESILIENT!!!

Lesson Principles:

1. Resilience is the ability to return to your original form after being bent or stretched. Know that you possess this quality.

2. Reflection is a powerful tool. Use it to remind yourself of what you have already endured.

3. Know that no matter what you may face, you are already victorious through Christ Jesus.

Let's Pray:

Father, in the name of Jesus, I thank You that in my moments of weakness You are my strength. I thank You that no matter what comes my way, I know that I have the victory through Christ Jesus. Continue to shape me, mold me and make me into the resilient woman that You have predestined me to be. In Jesus' name. Amen.

Lesson 3:

"Protect Your Energy"

"Respect yourself enough to walk away from anything that no longer serves you, grows you, or makes you happy." (anon)

I absorb energy like a sponge. Knowing this about myself has made it very easy for me to detach from anything or anyone that threatens my peace and joy. If you're a person like me that loves people, you understand this lesson was difficult at first. I didn't want to hurt anyone's feelings, so this was a truth that took me quite a while to embrace. There are those that will understand and respect your decision to create distance. Then you will have the ones that become offended. The fact of the matter is, it's difficult for people to accept what they don't understand or agree with. This was also a difficult lesson for me to learn. Yet, it turned out to be one of the most liberating.

Before I understood the principle of detaching, I would always allow people to linger in my personal space. Let me explain what I mean. People would call me or come to my home saying they wanted advice. I would drop everything to be there for them, listening attentively. After hours of dumping their weight on me I would passionately share with them what I saw from my perspective of the situation. They would then leave feeling free, while I would be emotionally and spiritually drained. The worst part is

NOTHING WOULD CHANGE!! These kinds of people just want someone to dump their issues and negativity on, so they can temporarily feel better. They come disguised as clients, friends and even family members. They come to you knowing full well they have no intentions on changing.

It took a minute for me to catch on, but once I got it, it was a wrap! Now, they all get one of two things from me. One is a listening ear and a closed mouth or a response of, "Nope, I'm not available." No apology or explanation is given. I refuse to sacrifice my time or wellbeing anymore. I pray for them, wish them the best and keep a healthy distance. At the end of the day, you must do what's best for you.

Pay attention to how people make you feel and respond accordingly. Even if that means creating distance. If you're not at your best, nothing or no one in your life will get your best. At all cost, protect YOUR energy!!

Lesson Principles:

1. Pay attention to the way things and people make you feel.
2. Create healthy boundaries for yourself with situations and people that drain your positive energy.
3. Don't be apologetic about protecting yourself.

Let's Pray:

Lord, help me to discern when to listen and when to speak and create healthy boundaries that protect my peace while still maintaining godly love for your people. In Jesus' name. Amen.

LESSON 4:

"Anger is an Unproductive Emotion"

"To be angry is to revenge the faults of others on ourselves." (Alexander Pope)

As a young child I was truly a character! Being the baby of six I was spoiled by everyone, but never a disrespectful brat. Mommy and daddy didn't play that temper tantrum mess; they would've been on me like white on rice! I was bold, outspoken, vivacious and charismatic. I was always smiling and laughing and would talk to anyone. I was straight forward and extremely honest. I said exactly what was on my mind which landed me in hot water more times than I care to remember. Nevertheless, this is who I was in my purest state.

As bright and promising as my adolescent years were, my transition from teen into adulthood was extremely difficult. Harsh experiences changed me. Life certainly has a way of doing that; it changes you. Bad relationships, broken friendships, betrayal, lies and abuse; it all played a part in altering my personality. No longer was I the bubbly, joyful little girl that would talk to anyone. I'd become guarded, untrusting and defensive. My smiles and laughter were traded for side-eyes and frowns. The negativity and hurt I held in my heart, over time, evolved into anger. That anger eventually became uncontrollable rage.

Whenever I tell my testimony about being delivered from anger, there are always puzzled faces in the audience. If anger has never been a struggle for you, it's difficult to comprehend. Anger and rage lead to reacting, instead of responding (we'll talk about that in a later chapter). It alters your ability to think rationally. You're unable to foresee the consequences of your words and actions. Honestly, in that moment, you don't really care. It creates the illusion that you are bigger, tougher and stronger than whomever or whatever it is that has angered you; which most times just is not the case.

After my marriage ended with my children's father, I found myself in yet another extremely tumultuous relationship. Everything we did was about the adrenaline rush, including pissing one another off; pushing buttons intentionally. By this point I'd been so much, I refused to allow any disrespect to go unanswered. If it was a fight you wanted, a fight you would get. He would yell at me, I would yell louder. Curse at me, I would use words in ways he never thought of. You touch me, I'd use whatever I could grab to break your hands. This went on for years!

It was Memorial weekend when our relationship

took a turn for the worse. Both of our birthdays were in May, so usually we would celebrate all month long. We'd gone to South Beach to hang out. We ate, drank and partied all day and into the afternoon. Finally, at about 5:00, we decided to leave so we could beat the heavy traffic exiting the beach. We got into the car to head home and at some point, an argument ensued. I can't even remember what it was about. What I do know is I'd had enough. I was so angry it felt as if the blood vessels in my eyes were about to burst. We were northbound on Interstate 95, traveling about 70 mph in the middle lanes; he was driving my car. I looked over at him and calmly said, "Get out." He chuckled and kept driving which infuriated me even more. Still looking at him I said again, "Get out of my car." This time he looked back. He seemed to be a bit shaken. "Do you see where we are?!?" he yelled. "I don't care where we are. Get out!!!"

Without a second thought, I shifted the gears of the car to park and turned the engine off. There we sat.... in the middle of the highway... in a parked vehicle. He was FRANTIC and I... I felt empowered!! The more he yelled and displayed panic, the stronger I felt. Finally, I have the upper hand. Finally, I am unafraid. Finally, I WIN!! Suddenly a car slams into us, pushing us forward at least a quarter of a mile. The impact throwing me into the windshield and shattering the entire rear window.

Immediately I was jolted from my power trip and forced to face the immediate consequences of my rage. I had lacerations to the face, swelling and burns on my arms and chest due to the airbags being deployed. There were large pieces of glass lodged in my back from the rear window. As I sat on the side of the road being treated by fire rescue, I knew I should've been dead. That day I walked away from that accident AND the relationship!

As you can see, it took extreme measures for me to realize reacting out of anger was not the answer. I must be honest and say although I never went that far again, it still took many years for me to get my anger under control. My work has been both mental and spiritual. I spent a year in counseling where I learned to not only recognize my triggers, but also purposely implement healthy ways to respond to them. Spiritually, my greatest developmental tool has been prayer. Prayer ignites the gift of Holy Spirit within me. Even when provoked, He gives me the mental capacity and ability to pause, breathe and exercise the restraint necessary. To this day I'm very careful to obey the word being swift to hear, slow to speak and slow to anger. Tests come regularly, but I allow the joy of the Lord to always be my strength.

Lesson Principles:

1. Do not allow anything outside of you to control your emotions.
2. Remain connected to God through prayer and studying the Word.
3. When you do feel yourself becoming upset, control your breathing. Deep breaths allow you to calm down and think instead of reacting out of your emotions!

Let's Pray:

Father in the name of Jesus, You said in Your Word in James 1:19," Be quick to hear, slow to speak and slow to anger." God You also said the joy of the Lord is my strength. God my prayer is that You would fill me with Your joy, so that I will be strong enough to withstand and not react to the attacks of the enemy. In Jesus' name. Amen.

LESSON 5:

"Perfectionism is an Illusion"

"I am careful not to confuse excellence with perfection. Excellence, I can reach for; perfection is God's business."
(Michael J. Fox)

I believe it was November 1994, which was a Saturday, when myself, my four sisters and sister-in-law had our first quarterly Sister's Day. Since life had become so busy for everyone, a specific date was set aside every four months for us to have some quality time together. My sister-in-law lived about three hours away, so everyone agreed to travel to her for the first one. My parents were very strict with me growing up so aside from holidays I didn't see my sisters very often. To say that I was excited to spend time with them is an understatement.

The day finally came, we decided to start our day with some shopping. The fact that I was 18 years old, with a new baby and working at Victoria's Secret left me with limited funds. For the most part I just watched them shop. It didn't matter, it was just nice to be around my sisters. That is until it was time for dinner.

Since we weren't familiar with the area, my sister-in-law picked the restaurant. We had a large party, but I remember being seated relatively quickly. We had been laughing and conversing all day about life, love, church, marriage, children, careers and everything else women chat about. Yet, when we sat down to eat, the conversation took an unexpected turn.

The conversation started with my siblings talking about how stern my dad was with them and how difficult it was for them to be in a singing group. This was not an uncommon topic of conversation when we all got together. However, listening to them reflect on him as a husband was very different. My sisters begin to candidly discuss the fact that our dad was not only physically abusive, he had also been unfaithful to our mother. I wasn't ready! Being the self-proclaimed poster child for daddy's girls all over the world, my dad was indeed my everything and could do no wrong in my eyes. To sit at that table and hear such harsh truths about him was, well, devastating.

I left that dinner with so many unspoken emotions. I was hurt, disappointed, angry, sad and confused. I felt as if I'd been given all this emotional junk to carry and no way to effectively deal with it. Because of the age gap between me and my sisters they felt more like mothers than siblings to me, so I didn't feel comfortable expressing my feelings to them at the time. I rode home in complete silence. Once I got home I wept uncontrollably. My heart was broken. Two significant things happened that day. First, I was forced to remove the imaginary pedestal of perfection I'd placed my father on for the last 18 years of my life. My mother always talked about the good, how he had a kind heart and worked so hard for his family. She would tell me how he courted her and promised her father he would take care of her. The image of a loving husband depicted to me in my mother's stories and modeled before me, was tainted. The second thing that happened was that I walked away from that conversation with a level of resentment towards my sisters. In my mind, not only did they not consider how revealing these facts about my daddy would affect me, but they hadn't given my brokenness a safe place to land. I can see now that I wasn't fair to my sisters because I held back how I felt. They were just discussing what was public knowledge for them. Yet, their public knowledge, for me, temporarily became an unbearable reality.

I carried the pain of that moment around with me for many years. To this day I've never even told my parents what I know. And I was afraid if I voiced it to anyone else, I would be putting their perception of my father in jeopardy. It wasn't until I gave my life to Christ and began to study His Word that I truly came to grips with the truth that NONE OF

US ARE PERFECT! Romans 3:23 proclaims, "All have sinned and come short of the glory of God" and we have all been gifted grace and mercy through Christ Jesus. I had to learn that we fail God every single day and He chooses to forgive us and expects that we do the same for one another.

The standard of perfection that I expected of my family and myself almost cost me a lifetime of joy and peace. Refusing to accept flaws in others made it extremely difficult to accept them within myself. I had to literally pray for God to cleanse my heart, renew my mind, and teach me to love myself and others as purely as He loves me, flaws and all.

Lesson Principles:

1. There is no perfect human being.

2. The goal is not to be perfect, but to serve a perfect God.

3. Extend the same grace to people, that God extends to you.

Let's Pray:

Father, in the name of Jesus, I thank you for helping me understand that we have all sinned and come short of your glory. I pray that You would help me to love myself as you love me and help me to extend the same grace to others, as You do to me. Knowing that I fail You every day, help me to forgive often and love unconditionally. In Jesus' name. Amen.

LESSON 6:

"Confidence is Necessary for Success"

"Be humble in your confidence, yet courageous in your character."
(Melanie Koulouris)

Confidence, there are different definitions for it. My personal favorite is a *feeling of self-assurance arising from one's appreciation of one's own abilities or qualities*. Confidence: belief and trust in my own personal ability to accomplish whatever I put forth my hands to do and the qualities that made me stand out from the rest. Confidence was never an issue for me. At least not until I began to operate in ministry. Suddenly, my confidence had become a fleeting dream, a thing of the past, an anomaly, nowhere to be found!

When I became a preacher, I started questioning and second guessing everything that made me so sure about myself in the first place. How can I speak to Your people? What will I say? Why will they listen to me? What about my mistakes? I'm just not equipped for this task! I learned relatively quickly that however you see yourself is how people will see you. I only saw flaws, failures, weaknesses and inabilities so that is what people began to see in me. All that I attempted to do when it came to ministry, was filtered through my lack of confidence.

This feeling intensified as I prepared to be the keynote

speaker at my own women's conference. I'd hosted the conference two years prior, but this would be my first time speaking. I was scared to death. For at least four months prior to the event I tried to convince God (yes God) that this was a grave mistake. I remember having extremely candid prayer time asking God if He was certain that He wanted *me* to speak. I compared myself to the speakers from previous years and even the potential speakers I wanted to contact for this conference. The voice of fear kept trying to convince me how much more equipped, knowledgeable, well prepared and qualified they were for the task. They already had a following and a presence. The mere thought of standing in that pulpit sent me into distress. In my mind, they were everything I wasn't; mentally I was already defeated. I was so desperate, I even asked my husband if he would stand in my place. I knew full well that answer would be a big fat no!

As the date approached, anxiety began to set in. One morning I was driving to work and having my usual conversation with God. I shared with Him all of my fears and concerns. It was during this prayer God reminded me exactly who He is and who I am in Him.

"Before I formed you in the womb I knew you, before you were born I set you apart; I appointed you as a prophet to the nations."

Jeremiah 1:5 (KJV)

"For I know the plans I have for you," declares the LORD, "plans to prosper you and not to harm you, plans to give you hope and a future."

Jeremiah 29:11 (KJV)

"For God has not given us a spirit of fear, but of power and of love and of a sound mind."

2 Timothy 1:7 (KJV)

"My grace is sufficient for you, for My strength is made perfect in weakness."

2 Corinthians 12:9 (KJV)

It was my confidence in God, my belief in *His* power and who *He* created me to be that would sustain me on WHATEVER platform He saw fit to place me. My success was no longer simply predicated on how well I speak, or dress or the gifts I possess. My success is solely based on who God is in my life and my ability to exercise faith in Him and exude confidence in the woman He created me to be. As I stood behind that podium, *LaShawn* disappeared and Christ rose up in me. SWAGG 2016 became a defining moment in my personal ministry. God showed Himself mightily to His women and He chose me as His vessel for which I am forever humbled and grateful. This experience proves that God delivers all that you need!

You will never be successful in the assignment that God has for you to fulfill, without total trust and 100% full belief in Him! It is in Him that we live, move and have our being. Without Him we are absolutely nothing, but with Him we are MORE than conquerors. Just believe!!!

Lesson Principles:

1. Know who God, the Father, is in your life.
2. Know who you are through Jesus Christ.
3. Place your confidence in God in all that you do.

Let's Pray:

Father, in the name of Jesus, I thank You for the perfect plan and purpose that You have for my life. I believe by faith that I am exactly who You say that I am, and I will accomplish all that You have created me to do. It is You that has begun a good work in me and I know that You will complete it. In Jesus' name. Amen.

LESSON 7:

"Your Actions Are Your Responsibility"

"When you blame others, you give up your power to GROW." (Anon)

This lesson brings me to the infamous Golden Rule: "Treat others how you want to be treated." This has been taught to me in some capacity probably since kindergarten. I must be honest and say, like many other lessons, this is much easier said than done. It just seems more than fair to mirror whatever treatment is being given to you. Obviously, this is how the other person should be treated, whether they want it or not.

I mean if someone is rude, disrespectful, lies, cheats, manipulates, or is just plain mean, my logic said they needed to know what that feels like. Right? Well, this is the approach I took for many years. From friendships to romantic relationships, however you treated me was exactly what you would get back and it worked for me. Until one day one I was venting to one of my sisters about another family member. I explained how extremely condescending she had been towards me and how I felt her antics were intentional. I told my sister I was tired of being silent and felt it was time she got a taste of her own medicine.

I went on with my rant while my sister listened attentively. I was so angry that she couldn't get a word in edgewise, even if she wanted to. Once I calmed she looked at me and said, "Baby sis, I understand how you feel, but repeating that behavior isn't going to help the situation." I wanted to say, "I DON'T CARE! I just want her to feel the way she makes other people feel." but out of respect, I remained quiet let her finish. "No, the way that she interacts with us sometimes is not right." She must have felt the heat coming from my head!! "Just know," she continued, "Your actions are your responsibility."

It was another one of those statements that immediately commanded my attention. "What do you mean?" I asked. She continued, "You're a reflection of God first. Don't ever be so consumed with making a point or getting even with someone, that you mishandle the moment or especially the person. God is going to hold you accountable for what *you* do or don't do, not what is done to you." I was immediately convicted in my heart.

As Christians, we can never become so enthralled with what people do to us, that we forget our purpose on Earth which is ultimately to please God. Every thought, every deed, every response (both verbal and nonverbal), is our responsibility. What we do, say and think will either warrant a reward or echo a judgment into eternity.

Think beyond the here and now. Be the salt and light of the Earth that God intended for His people to be. Be the exception and stay positive at all cost. In doing this you will evoke the change that you want to see, one person at a time!

Lesson Principles:

1. What you do is what you will either be rewarded for or judged by in eternity.
2. Always focus on how you can make a positive impact, even in a negative situation.
3. As Christians, our responsibility is to be the salt and the light of the World.

Let's Pray:

Father, in the name of Jesus, it is not always easy to remain positive when dealing with people. However, we realize Your Word commands us to love one another as we love ourselves. God, we ask that You would help us to love one another with an Agape love. Let all that we do, say, and think be filtered through that love. In Jesus' name we pray. Amen.

Lesson 8:

"Peace is Priceless"

"And the peace of God, which transcends all understanding, will guard your hearts and your minds in Christ Jesus."
(Philippians 4:7)

It was my 25th birthday when I woke up as I do every birthday, excited about what this day would hold for me. To my surprise there was a big beautiful gift bag sitting on the edge of my bed. I jumped up, grabbed the bag and began to pull out the contents. There was a sexy navy blue, bronze and white dress with matching bronze open toe heels. There was also a card at the bottom of the bag. In it was money and instructions for me to have my hair, nails, and feet done. Gift number one was a success.

It was about 7:00 pm and I was all dolled up and ready to celebrate! We took the kids to my mom's house and he (my ex-husband) whisked me off for a surprise night on the town. I remember having butterflies in my stomach and smiling from ear to ear. Once we arrived at the secret location, I realized it was a popular jazz lounge in Ft. Lauderdale that I'd been wanting to visit for months. He shut it down for a private celebration for me with our closest friends. Gift number two was amazing.

It was beautifully decorated like a spot straight out of the Harlem Renaissance era. The lights were low, and every table was lit by individual candlelight. There was a live band and singer that played great music all night long. The food smelled amazing and my favorite cake was on display. Along with all of that, there was a collection of beautiful gifts specifically picked out with me in mind. Right there, in that moment, surrounded by my wonderful friends, creating fond memories, I was happy.

I waited until I got home to open my presents. It had become a tradition (that I keep to this day) to sit in the middle of my bed like a big kid and read my cards first and then unwrap my gifts. I'm a wordsmith so cards were always very important to me. To me, they reveal more of what's in your heart than the actual gift. As I read each card and then unwrapped each gift, I was overwhelmed by all the genuine love I felt. Of course, I saved the box with his name on it for last. It was a plain brown box and a little heavy. I took my time peeling back the tape that held the flaps of the box in place. Once I finally got it open, there staring back at me was a Glock 9mm pistol. I was mesmerized. For years we talked about it, but for various reasons we never made a purchase. He said he thought it would be a good idea to buy it for my protection. Little did either of us know the one I would need protection from was him!

It had been less than four months since my birthday.

As I lay on that same bed, bleeding from my leg and arm, unable to escape from the grasp of his hands around my neck, I thought about *that* birthday gift. Gasping for air, I reached back over my head to the night stand where I kept my gun. Suddenly, he released my neck, grabbed his keys and left the house. I can't really say to this day if he knew what I was reaching for, but I'm grateful to God for the outcome.

The house, the cars, the financial stability, the temporary moments of happiness, the persona of perfection and even elaborate gifts kept me in a volatile situation for almost ten years. Dysfunction and abuse became my new normal. I knew at that point no amount of money would ever be able to purchase the one thing I needed the most, that was peace. Peace in my heart, peace in my mind, peace in my spirit and peace in my life.

I was under the misconception that removing myself from the marriage would bring me that peace. I did what I thought would assist me in moving past the traumas of my marriage into a life of contentment. But truthfully, that quality of life couldn't be attained under my own power. I continued to find myself in tumultuous situation after situation, void of the very serenity I so desperately desired. Five years later when I was invited to church by a coworker, that one encounter quenched a thirst in me I wasn't even aware existed. That Sunday a genuine passion for Christ was ignited. Immediately I made a choice that the next relationship I would pursue would be with *Him*! I spent time with Him. I talked with Him and listened to Him. I learned about Him and what He requires of me through His Word. In exchange, God became the source of peace in my life; peace that surpasses all understanding. I now know through His Word, if I keep my mind fixed on Him, He will keep me in perfect peace. A peace that is not predicated on the things that are going on around me or the difficulties of life.

    The peace of God is a perpetual gift that you too can possess. It is available to you every single day of your life. Make the choice today to get to know God for yourself. You are His child and He is patiently waiting for you. The gift of peace is an expression of His love for you. Accept this gift today.

Lesson Principles:

1. Peace is one of life's most essential necessities.
2. You will never obtain true peace without a relationship with God.
3. His peace will continue to add value to your life daily.

Let's Pray:

Lord, I thank You for the gift of peace that surpasses all understanding and guards my heart and my mind through Your Son Jesus Christ. I pray that others will see the benefit of Your peace through my life and they will be drawn to develop a true relationship with You. In Jesus' name I pray. Amen.

LESSON 9:

"Be You"

"Be the most authentic and genuine version of yourself, unapologetically."
(LaShawn Spry)

If you're anything like me, there are levels to your personality. For instance, when I am in a business setting, my ratchet side is fully tamed for obvious reasons. When I'm meeting people for the first time, even in a social setting, I am purposely more subdued than if I were with those that have known me for years. This isn't a misrepresentation of who I really am. On the contrary, it's just a more toned-down version of my true self. It's simply being cognizant of your current surroundings. This is very similar to what is called code switching. Code Switching is defined as the process of shifting from one language to another, depending on the social context or conversational setting. However, when we choose to completely change our character or alter personality traits to suit a person or group of people in our space at that moment, there's something very wrong with that.

Let me give you some clearer examples. Have you ever pretended to be kind hearted, when you're mean natured? Ever tried to come across as very affectionate, knowing you're quite reserved? A lot of us are guilty of this one: claiming to be thick-skinned and not easily offended, then time reveals us to be both super sensitive and quickly irritated. What you don't realize is there is no way to create a sound foundation to build solid relationship when you're meeting people with your *representative.* Your *representative* is who you want people to think you are, instead of just being your true self.

A *defense mechanism* is what I used to call it. I was protecting myself from being judged by people who didn't stick around long enough to get to know me; at least that's what I made myself believe. Despite my unwillingness to be real, I expected authenticity from everyone I met. Some nerve, right?!?!?! No matter what my desires were, I kept meeting people that were just as guarded and dishonest about who they truly were as I was.

Sometimes we do so much in the name of "protecting self" that we don't even see that we're doing more damage in the end. At the time I didn't recognize that the people I attracted were reflecting an image to me that I was giving them. Even though I said nothing, I wound up attracting who I was and not who I pretended to be. With this method I would never be able to connect with the people intended for my life. All I was doing was misrepresenting myself and the beauty God purposely within.

Not only that, what was I saying to God about the woman *He* created me to be?! What message did my phoniness send about the characteristics and traits that *He* placed within me? To a God that, *"formed my inward parts; wove me in my mother's womb. Fearfully <u>and wonderfully made me.</u>"* (Psalms 139:13-14a) Every time we pretend to be someone else, we're really saying to our Creator the woman that You designed and predestined me to be does not meet my standards. Is that really the message you want to send God?? One of thanklessness and ingratitude?? For me the answer is absolutely NOT !!!

I had to embrace the truth that God made no mistakes when He created me. My love for Him and the fact that I wanted the world to emulate truth to me meant it was my responsibility to start being the woman God made me to be. This was no easy feat. To achieve authenticity, I had to be willing to commit to being real, even when it became uncomfortable. To receive truth, I had to share my ugly truth. To be given transparency, I had to be ready to give it. The things I saw that I didn't like about me, I had the power and the courage change! It's called personal growth and self-development.

Not everyone is going to like you. I promise that's cool because God didn't create you to be connected to everybody! Think about the lives of those that are counting on you; waiting on you to be brave enough, so they can glean from your strength. The few that are depending on you to show up and change the circumference of their entire existence. They will ask themselves, if she went through that and was still able to make it out and change that about herself, then what makes my situation any different?

There are people in this world that need you. They need your authenticity. They need your courage. They even need your faults, flaws and failures and testimony of triumphs! Truth is we are all imperfect beings unconditionally loved by a perfect God. Be you, not just for self, but to help liberate those connected to you and ultimately bring honor and glory to God!

Lesson Principles:

1. The world needs your most authentic self.

2. God made no mistakes when He created you.

3. Be you, authentically and unapologetically; those who mind don't matter and those that matter, won't mind.

Let's Pray:

Father in the name of Jesus, we first say thank You for loving us enough to take the time to fearfully and wonderfully make us. Now we ask that You help us to see ourselves, the way You see us, as Your carefully crafted Masterpiece. In Jesus' name. Amen.

Lesson 10:

"Vulnerability is Necessary"

"Vulnerability is the birthplace of love, belonging, joy, courage, empathy, and creativity. It is the source of hope, empathy, accountability, and authenticity. If we want greater clarity in our purpose or deeper and more meaningful spiritual lives, vulnerability is the path." (Brené Brown)

Once you've endured so much in life, especially at the hands of those closest to you, protecting yourself becomes second nature. Building walls and safe guarding your heart with emotional barbed wire seems to be more of a responsibility, than mere choice. You develop a hard exterior in hopes that it keeps those with intentions to prey on your weaknesses at bay. Hiding your smile, scarcely sharing personal details about yourself, and rarely making new connections becomes the norm. You skirt through life cautiously, skeptically, alone.

Guarded and isolated is how I spent almost 14 years of my adult life. I was determined to have just enough control in my relationships, so that no one would get close enough to hurt me. I maintained just the right amount of leverage that if I saw anything remotely familiar to abuse or deception, I was able to get the heck out of dodge without feeling a thing. That is if I didn't choose the vindictive route and get you before you got me.

I didn't realize that as much as I attempted to block negativity from my life, I blocked just as much good. The protective barriers I'd built mentally and emotionally not only sheltered me from the failure I feared in forming relationships, but also hindered me from the possibility of any type of success. Unfortunately, while I had my best interest at heart, the reality was that overtime, I had done myself a major disservice. If I was ever going to experience the quality interaction I so desperately desired with another human being, I would have to become comfortable with the discomfort of vulnerability.

For someone like me having been through what I'd been through and being exposed to the depths of deceit, dysfunction and distrust as both receiver and giver; you might as well use profane language rather than talk to me about being vulnerable! In my eyes it was the equivalent of opening myself up to the possibility of being disappointed repeatedly with little hope of recovery. Truthfully, this is the long and short of being vulnerable. Yet the beauty is, you can't have anything good without it.

Even after I understood all of this, it was still a *major* challenge for me, but I decided to give it a try. So, I opened myself up to a fresh new friendship with a young lady I met in church. She was very welcoming, intelligent, and funny. She had a great career, gorgeous home, solid marriage, and most importantly she loved the Lord. What better person to take a chance on, right? I jumped into this friendship with both hands and feet (mistake number one).

While I was determined to live beyond my relational downfalls, this newly developed friendship became my sole focus. I refused to let my past failures in this area of my life control its outcome. I found myself completely open and vulnerable to what appeared to be the possibility of a great relationship. Little did I know this connection was positioning me to learn, yet another very valuable lesson.

We planned a girl's trip to the Bahamas for my birthday. I was super excited because it would've been the first stamp on my passport *and* we planned to cross off a bucket list item which was swimming with the dolphins (in my case it would've been floating because I can't swim). I saved up and planned my birthday vacation around this trip, so it would be a memorable one. Well, just a few days before we had our first disagreement. This didn't scare me because I understood any strong relationship had the ability to withstand some storms. Apparently, I was the only one of us that felt this way because later that evening our trip was canceled. At first, I was completely thrown for a loop because I didn't think anything was said or done to warrant that response. As the hours passed and the reality of the loss began to sink in, I became angry! *"This is why I don't let people in!"*, I reminded myself. I can't lie, I was thrown into a tailspin of emotions. These emotions, thoughts and feelings played out over several months. I even tried to salvage the friendship. Ultimately, I concluded that I had no regrets about being open, rather it wasn't wise to be open to a person that wasn't willing to take the same risks. And these are truths that are only revealed over time.

From the very beginning, I felt this friendship had the potential to grow into something beautiful and lasting, but I was missing one important principle that I needed to grasp prior to pursuing any new relationships. A key component in having vulnerability work in your favor is consulting God. Proverbs 3:5-6 (NLT) says, *"Trust in the Lord with all your heart; do not depend on your own understanding. Seek His will in all you do, and He will show you which path to take."* Ask God to reveal *His* desire for every person that comes into your life. Pray that He will reveal their heart and intentions to you. Truth is, when we consult God about every decision and every relationship, He will ensure that we make choices that are both pleasing to

Him and in our best interest. When our decisions please God we have nothing to fear or worry about because, *"We know that God causes everything to work together for the good of those who love God and are called according to His purpose."* (Romans 8:28 NLT) Even if our connections don't evolve into the picture *we* create in our minds, we are still perfectly content with God's will for our lives. This creates a most conducive atmosphere for vulnerability to flourish.

Vulnerability is a choice. You must make the conscious decision to leave yourself open to life's possibilities; whether it's the probability of being hurt or healing. It includes the being susceptible to the hurt of a vicious lie or covered by a sincere truth. There is the risk of stagnation or the potential to flourish. The likelihood of intense heartache or exposure to unconditional love. All things in life, both tragic and beautiful, are cultivated within our connection to others. Without vulnerability, we negate the power of human connection. Social worker Brene' Brown says, "Connection is why we're here. It's what gives purpose and meaning to our lives." "Without vulnerability, we have no connection." "Without connection, we won't have relationship with one another." Without one another, we have nothing."

Lesson Principles:

1. Vulnerability is being open to whatever life has to offer.
2. Vulnerability is the pathway to all life's treasures.
3. Our relationship with God gives us the courage to be vulnerable and still feel protected.

Let's Pray:

Lord, I thank You for the gift of vulnerability. I pray that You would equip me with the faith to trust Your direction for my life and the courage to walk my process boldly, knowing that no weapon formed against me shall prosper and You work all things together for my good! In Jesus' name. Amen.

Lesson 11:

"You're Stronger Than You Think"

"Strength and growth come only through continuous effort and struggle."
(Napoleon Hill)

I went from the sheltered Pentecostal *church girl* to the *promiscuous fun girl*. I made it through the embarrassment of a teenage pregnancy and being forced to become a young, ill-prepared bride. I finally escaped a riotous ten-year marriage filled with mental and physical abuse and ongoing infidelity by myself and my ex-husband. A nasty divorce played out for over almost two years which led to a horrible custody battle. After the divorce I bounced from one failed relationship to another, consistently. And to think, this isn't even half of my story!

I developed a skewed view of love along with an extremely distorted self-perception. Life had become one huge loss after another. It became increasingly difficult for me to function in the chaos of my current reality. My distraction of choice was alcohol. It became my numbing agent. Whenever the pressures of life became too great, the voices in my head too loud, or my heart too heavy, I drank until I was oblivious to it all. However, anyone who's ever picked up a habit to pacify a pain knows that feeling only paralyzes you for a moment. Once the anesthetic wears off, the agony of unavoidable truth is right there to greet you; most times it's more intense than before.

I was drowning in a vicious cycle of dysfunctional love, abuse, rage, and depression. I'd gotten tired of making myself physically sick just to wake up in the exact same mental and emotional state. I realized drinking and clubbing was merely a temporary fix and was making things worse. In my heart, I knew it was time to face the very thing I spent all these years running from. It was time to deal with the lies constructed by my past. I was ready to work on the woman I was created to be versus yielding to the tainted idea cultivated by years of purposeless relationships. To do that, I had to tap into my inner strength.

Here's what I discovered about inner strength, every pressurized situation I've ever been placed in, and there have been many, has always revealed to me a new layer of strength that I wasn't even aware I had. With every test that I passed and trial I survived, I learned more and more of my own inner strength. With every tragedy, even the ones I wished would have taken me out, I became more and more resilient.

Had it not been for the darkest days in my life, I would never have discovered the priceless gems hidden within by God Himself. As I begin to press the rewind button of my mind and recall the pain, disappointment, heartaches and difficulties I'd faced, I had to also acknowledge the fact that I was still standing! By looking back and shifting my focus, I uncovered an inner strength that I didn't recognize before. Strength to love myself and others; to endure life's most crucial moments. It allowed me the ability to persevere in my valley experiences and remain humble during my peaks and mountain top moments. And just as I did the work to discover mine, the same unyielding spirit lies within you!

Lesson Principles:

1. God has already given you the strength you need for your journey.
2. No external force can replace your inner strength.
3. True strength is revealed in life's most difficult moments.

Let's Pray:

Father, in the name of Jesus, Your Word declares that, "I can do all things through Christ which strengthens me." (Philippians 4:13) I pray that You would help me to keep this truth at the forefront of my mind especially during life's darkest, most challenging tests. In Jesus' name. Amen.

LESSON 12:

"Know Your True Identity"

"Unlike a drop of water which loses its identity when it joins the ocean, man does not lose his being in the society in which he lives. Man's life is independent. He is born not for the development of the society alone, but for the development of his self." (B.R. Ambedkar)

Statistics say one in every four women will become victims of intimate partner violence in her lifetime. I learned the hard way, I was one of them. It was November 2010 when I stood in my closet getting ready for my grandmother's wake. I found myself lost in a sea of weighted, depressing thoughts. You would think these were the obvious feelings of grief because I was preparing to say my final goodbyes to my 95-year old grandmother. Surprisingly, this wasn't grief at all. I was experiencing feelings of fear and anxiety because my ex-husband would be there.

For years he served as a source of not only physical, but mental abuse. Although the marriage had been dissolved for years at this point, the effects of the torment and mistreatment I suffered still mentally affected me. He had become the very bane of my existence. The mere thought of being in close proximity to this man forced me right back into an extremely dark mental space.

The shame of being pregnant at 17 years old and unmarried left me in a vulnerable place. I was susceptible to being deceived by the lies of the enemy and that's exactly what began to happen. Amidst a foundation of brokenness, a tower of lies was built. Very quickly after we said *I do,* the bullying began. I was made to feel as if he were superior to me because of his financial security and educational background. He was well spoken, well dressed, already had a stable career, owned his car and secured bank accounts. He didn't need me. On the contrary, I was the one that needed him or, so I was convinced to believe.

The fact that I was fresh out of high school with a newborn and no job made it easy for him to play mental games. Fear effortlessly set in. I was afraid to leave or to defend myself against him. I didn't ask for help because I didn't want anyone to know what was really going on. I realize now he was a bully and intimidation was his weapon of choice. Suffering abuse at the hands of a man I planned to spend the rest of my life with literally rendered me powerless.

That day as I prepared for my grandmother's funeral, something within me snapped. This is where the power to face my abuser was ignited. I waged war against every lie he'd ever planted in my mind. The public shaming and bullying I had endured, harsh, cruel words with the intent to break me mentally and emotionally lit a fire in me. I experienced intimidation from a man that was supposed to love, protect and honor me, but instead left me mentally battered and at times in fear for my life! For years I allowed *his* brokenness and weakness to render me powerless, but not anymore.

I spent years peeling back the layers of deception and seeds of lies just to get to the root of who I really am. Standing in that closet I began to speak declaration of truth over myself. *"No longer will I be bullied or intimidated by any other human being. You don't have the right to treat me like I'm inferior in any way, shape or form. I will never give another person the opportunity to feel that they make or break me. I have given all my broken pieces to the Potter who made me and continues to mold me into the picture of perfection that He has always seen me as. I don't have to live in fear of you or what you threaten to do to me. For my God has not given me the spirit of fear, but of power and of love and of a sound mind. You don't get to render me powerless. For I serve a God that has all power in His hands and as His child that same power dwells within me."*

It wasn't until I forged a strong relationship with God and learned who He is, that I started to comprehend my identity as His child. I am the daughter of a King; the apple of His eye. I am blessed and highly favored. I am fearfully and wonderfully made. I am the head and not the tail; the lender and not the borrower. I am a virtuous woman whose value is far above rubies. I am God's Masterpiece. By His stripes, I am healed. I am forgiven for all my sins. I am an overcomer and more than a conqueror. I am victorious in every situation and I am a new creature in Christ Jesus.

Once you are sure of the God that you serve, you, too, will become very clear about your identity in Him. Then you will have the ability to combat every lie with the truth of who God says you are!

Lesson Principles:

1. You can't combat a lie about yourself until you know your truth.
2. To know who you are, you must first know who God is.
3. You are who God says you are!

Let's Pray:

Lord, Your word is filled with truths of I am. Thank You for loving me unconditionally and desiring the best for me. Please help me to combat the lies of the enemy with the truth that You spoke over my life before I was formed in my mother's womb. In Jesus' name. Amen.

LESSON 13:

"It's Never Too Late"

"It's never too late to follow your dreams and there's no time like the present to start." (Anon)

One night my husband and I had the humbling opportunity of hosting a segment on *The Curve* internet radio show on www.yopodner.fm. For me, the experience was both mind-blowing and heart wrenching. I know that sounds like an oxymoron. Truth is as excited as I was for the favorable circumstances, I was just as consumed by the immediate thought that, at almost 40 years old, I have yet to completely walk in and live out my passion and purpose! My mind just kept repeating, "So much potential, so little time." How could I have allowed myself to waste so much time and miss so many opportunities? My thoughts became so loud on the ride home that I literally wanted to SCREAM!

Then it came to me, I've dedicated 18 years of my life to this career and now it's in my way. I'M DONE! I'm going to go out and make my dreams a reality. I'm going to stop talking about it and JUST DO IT! I have gifts and talents! I carry valuable information, from my knowledge and experiences that I can use to help powerful women live their very best lives. I'm not sitting on all that God has placed in me anymore. I looked over at my husband (He's always my go to person when my thoughts take off and leave me) I said, "Baby, I hate my job and I'm not going back. I'm going to pursue my purpose full time!" I gave him statistic after statistic. I named women who are doing it and successful at it. I reminded him of my gifts and passions, my creative ideas and the visions God placed in me. He lets me ramble on and on and on. Once I stop he says, "Baby, you never have to go back to a job you're not happy with. But how are you going to fund the vision? Don't you think it would be wise to strategically plan your transition?" There it was, just the reality check I needed.

There are times when the oddest things will set fire to our tail feathers. For me it was the approach of my 40th birthday. For you it could be the fear of missed opportunities, closed doors, mental stagnation or even watching someone else function successfully in a lane you desire to be in. Whatever the source of the spark, REFUSE TO BE CONSUMED! Use your desires as fuel to get you where you need to be! These are the steps we're going to take to get us there...

1. Be clear about your vision. Write it down and look at it EVERYDAY!

2. Develop a team that believes in you and your vision.

These are not necessarily friends, but people that can see what you see. They will sharpen your mind, push you to take risks, hold you accountable and help keep you focused.

3. Set realistic goals. Build a timeline and stick to it!

4. Create a strategic plan. Be clear about the steps you will need to take to achieve those goals.

5. Persevere past obstacles. Stay the course through tears, fears, doubts, concerns, naysayers, and folks' opinions. No matter what, keep going! QUITTING IS NOT AN OPTION.

6. Remain focused on the big picture. Keep the reason(s) you're pursuing your goals in sight. This will keep you motivated.

7. Put in the hard work. You won't accomplish anything merely talking and writing. Get up and get your grind on! Only then will others take you seriously.

8. Finally, pray and have faith until you see the fruits of your labor.

You're not alone in this. We all have that "Should've Could've Would've" syndrome at one point or another, but we don't have to stay there! God woke you up because He still has purpose within you! You haven't reached your full potential. You have yet to max out in this life. Though I took my husband's advice, implemented a plan and am so much further than I was before, I still have a long way to go. My career as a dispatcher has switched from a burden to a means of funding my dream! I am successfully birthing my vision, while maintaining the stability of a full-time career and furthering my education. Nobody, but God!!

So, for those of you that feel that you are still stuck, be encouraged. Know that our truth is *"it's never too late to be what you should've, could've, would've been!"* I pray this empowers you to be all that you were predestined to be and that you will in turn utilize your story to empower someone else.

Lesson Principles:

1. Never give up on your vision.
2. Don't live in a space of regret.
3. If it hasn't happened yet, there is still work to be done.

Let's Pray:

Lord, help us to continue to believe in the perfect plan and purpose You have mapped out for our lives. In Jesus' name. Amen.

LESSON 14:

"We Are Forever Becoming"

""He made you, you - on purpose. You are the only you - ever. Becoming ourselves means we are actively cooperating with God's intention for our lives, not fighting him or ourselves."
(Stasi Eldredge)

I am the baby girl of six children born to Margaret, who was a nurse and grade school teacher and Freddie who was a state worker and pastor. All five of my siblings were intelligent, talented and hard working. Each of them also developed a relationship with God at a young age. As you could probably imagine, being born into a family like this came with its own degree of pressure. There was pressure from my parents to meet the standards of respect, competence and independence. Then there was the pressure of meeting the expectations set for me by my older siblings. Let's not forget the pressure placed on me by church folks based solely on the fact that I was a preacher's kid. Lastly, there was the pressure I placed on myself not to let anyone down. Sometimes I wonder if any of us took into consideration the fact that God had my path mapped out before I was ever even thought about.

Anyway, as you can probably already imagine I folded under all the pressure. Every bar I'd reach for, instead of obtaining it, the further out of reach it seemed. The more I'd attempt to please everyone and make them proud of me, the more miserably I'd fail. The more I failed, the more comfortable I'd become with the title of being a failure. When my parents, siblings, and the church seemed to set unattainable standards for me, the rest of the world seemed to embrace me exactly as I was. Bad decisions, flaws, and failures didn't seem to matter. It looked as if I could be my imperfect self, with no pressure. So, I stopped trying to please church and family and began pleasing the world, not realizing this was all part of God's ultimate plan for my life.

From the age of 15 until about 31 I intentionally rebelled. Every expectation set for me and boundary placed on me, I ignored. Once I left my parents' home, in my mind, I finally escaped the pressure I lived under for 18 years of my life; that kept me feeling inadequate and suppressed. I made it my business to go as far left as I possibly could. Everything they said don't do, I did. Everywhere they said don't go, I went. I pushed the envelope, went against the grain, and ruffled feathers. That's what I was good at. I wasn't good at following the path already set; the one everyone thought I should. I wasn't like everyone else and I was comfortable with that. At this point I resolved in my mind that I had to blaze my own trail. Where their journey was straight, mine would be crooked. Where theirs seemed smooth, my process was going to be rocky and bumpy; I was fine with it.

When I finally gave my life to Christ, I was initially ashamed of my process and the path I'd chosen in life. I didn't want to expose the things I'd been through or done. However, as I learned the power of grace and mercy I became stronger and more confident in my own skin. The truth is, God kept me! He was the reason I was still alive and this knowledge gave my process power. I realized every part of my story was necessary, every detail intentional. God used my past faults, failures and flaws to assist me in becoming the virtuous woman that He created me to be.

Little did I know God would use me to do something new. All my past experiences were just part of the process of creating *Forever Becoming*; a blueprint for imperfect vessels like me, to follow. God knew that there would be an entire group of us, across the world, that may fail under the expectations of man. Yet, those human failures in the eyes of God, translate into *Forever Becoming* which became a way of life, a means to choose every single day to be...

1. Brave

2. Exquisite

3. Confident

4. Optimistic

5. Motivated

6. Intentional

7. of Noble Character

8. a Goal Digger

This is not a process of perfection, nor is it about meeting the expectations and bars set for you by man. It is for the sole purpose of always striving towards and choosing to be the woman that God created and called you to be. It's a blueprint to assist us in fulfilling His plan and purpose for our lives, with the ultimate goal of leaving this world completely empty.

Lesson Principles:

1. Every day is another opportunity to be the woman you were created to be.

2. Adopt a lifestyle rooted in morals and values that mirror the life you want to create for yourself.

3. Fearlessly pursue the greatest version of yourself every day!

Let's Pray:

Lord, the word says that I am a new creature in Christ Jesus. Help me to believe that truth and become all that You ordained for me to be. Help me to accomplish the good works that You have set for me to do on earth. May all the glory in my life ultimately go to You! In Jesus' name. Amen.

LESSON 15:

"Your Vision Creates Your Reality"

"The only thing worse than being blind is having sight, but no vision." (Helen Keller)

Have you ever had the pleasure (or utter gloom, depending on how you perceive them) of meeting a dreamer? You know the kind of people I'm talking about. The ones that have a precise picture in their minds eye of the exact way their lives should be. I mean, from career to the car they'll drive, the house they will own and the neighborhood in which the house should be built. They know the amount of money they want to make and the kind of person they will share it with (oh yeah, we really are that detailed). Dreamers have a vivid imagination and picture of their fantasy life which makes operating in the day to day mundane of real life somewhat difficult and for some it can be downright depressing. On the other hand, the beauty of a dreamer is that they are very much in tune with their inner desires and hopes. They are also very rarely driven by the almighty dollar. Instead, it is passion and desire that drives them. They are motivated to live out their dream. Yet most times, they have no concept of HOW to attain it!

Just in case you're wondering what makes me such a "know it all" when it comes to the dreamer, I myself am one!! As far back as I can remember my life was GRAND...in my mind anyway. As a matter of fact, I lived life more peacefully in my mind than I ever did in the real world. I also recognized at an early age that my perception of life was very different from those around me. I knew that I was special (in a good way, lol) and I possessed some unique characteristics and gifts that would eventually make me great. While all of this was fantastic, at 39 years old I realized not many things in my life matched the picture I'd created for myself. The question then became, "What am I missing?"

I began an intense self-examination process. I picked apart my thoughts, actions, my work ethic as well as my focus. I then started to study the people I considered to be successful. People that were already living the life I wanted for myself. I found these people started with a dream, but unlike me, they didn't stop there. Every successful person had vision! They created a clear picture of what they wanted to accomplish, wrote it down on paper, and then developed a step by step plan to make it happen. While the vision is your *what*, (meaning what it is that you are working towards); strategy becomes your how, (the way that you will make it happen). The moment you have a clear picture of where you're going and how you're going to get there, you stop merely being a dreamer and you become a visionary!

Understand, while every visionary has a dream, not every dreamer is a visionary. If you want to live the life you've created in your mind and heart, simply having the dream is not enough. You must have a clear and precise picture of what it is you want to accomplish and be able to clearly articulate that to your team. Yes, I said team! Contrary to popular belief, no one successfully executes alone. And the last step is delegation and implementation.

I must be honest and say you will still have those moments when you'll slip back into the abyss of *dreamville*. However, now your visits will be very different. You will grab the dream and intentionally follow the steps needed to make it a reality. God will send you people that believe as deeply as you do. They will keep you motivated, encourage you, hold you accountable and help you do the work necessary to yield the results you long to see.

Lesson Principles:

1. Every success begins as a vision.

2. The difference between a vision and a dream is a calculated plan and hard work.

3. No one does it all alone.

Let's Pray:

Lord, You said in Your word without vision the people perish. God, we thank You for a clear vision of the work that You have for us to do in this life. Thank You for connecting us with people who will help us to make that vision our reality. In Jesus' name. Amen.

LESSON 16:

"Shift Your Focus"

"Don't exert so much energy into being disappointed, that you miss the blessing." (LaShawn Spry)

Reality: *the state of things as they exist, as opposed to an idealistic or notional idea of them.* In layman's terms, it is how things really *are* versus how you thought they would be. During those happy moments in your life when everything is going right, it can be almost euphoric. It'll have you seeing unicorns during the day and spitting neon colored glitter at night. (okay that's a bit much) A healthy perception of what truly exists settles you into a happy place where you're excited, content and full of life.

However, when things aren't so great, reality gets a bum rap. The facts of your situation will have you trapped in your feelings. Your hardships can hold you hostage in the useless realm of what you wish you had done differently. It can make you rethink every decision you've ever made! Let's be honest, the here and now is not always an easy season to live in. Yet, I have learned that it is *always* necessary. It is designed to give, destroy, teach, and build something that you will need moving forward. Chrystal Evans Hurst said this in an interview:

"Understand that small things matter. Many times, the small things don't matter to us like they really should. Once

you get past them you can look back and see that those small things were a part of God's plan. You don't realize it when you're in action."

All facets of time matter; the good, the bad, the great, the horrible, the extraordinary, the mediocre, and the painful. It is all essential and beneficial to your journey, the person you are to become and the assignment you are to fulfill. To survive strenuous periods of your journey *and* maintain your joy while in the process, you must learn to shift your focus.

When the idea of your current truth is skewed, this makes it almost impossible to see the good that is happening. The opportunity to grow, unveil a new level of joy, and discover untapped purpose could be present, but because you're so blinded by life's challenges, you can't see your blessings. We all know how our mind personifies adversity verses positivity. When experiences like rejection, heartache, and disappointment saturate your path, your line of vision becomes obscure. Whatever you concentrate on becomes your reality and you wind up creating the very situation or outcome that you so desperately wanted to escape or avoid.

Shifting your focus can feel like seeing for the very first time. It is amazing the things that become apparent when you intentionally change your center of attention from the negative to the positive. Things that were once invisible, suddenly become obvious. Learn to observe life through the lenses of faith, hope and gratitude. Believe that even in the darkest moments, good is still there. Once you recognize the good, you consciously begin to pursue it.

Listen, life happens, and hard times are unavoidable. You may not be able to control the exact moment you're in, but you always have the power to choose your point of focus. I urge you to make a deliberate effort to see your current conditions through the love and light that life has to offer. Maintain a positive mindset, especially during tests and trials. Life is comprised of millions of fleeting moments and hard times don't last forever. Focus on the good, learn from the rest and teach those that will follow you to do the same. I am praying for you.

Lesson Principles:

1. You are always focused on something, either good or bad. Intentionally choose the good.

2. View life through the lenses of faith, hope and gratitude.

3. Consciously pursue the good; it's there.

Let's Pray:

Father, in the name of Jesus there are times in life when reality becomes too much to bare, and it is difficult to keep our focus on the good. Help us to daily apply Colossians 3:2 which says, "Think about the things of heaven, not the things of earth." God ultimately, we want to fulfill the perfect plan and purpose that You have designed for our lives. Help us believe that every experience is pressing us closer and closer towards that mark. In Jesus' name. Amen.

Lesson 17:

"It's Still Fly to be a Lady"

"What attracts a man's attention doesn't always attract his respect. What turns a man's head doesn't always turn his heart." (Anon)

I shared a rare mommy/daughter day with my 19-year-old. Between work, school and her social life our one-on-one time is rare, yet still important, so we make it happen whenever we can. Anyway, as we sat there chatting and my baby is catching me up on everything that's been going on in her life, the strangest thing started to happen. I started to *see* her. (stay with me I'm going somewhere, lol) Okay, you remember the movie Avatar? (I know good and well ya'll said YES!) You know the part when Zoe Saldana's character *Neytiri* told her love interest, Jake, "I see you"?? Well, that's what I'm talking about. I wasn't just listening to her words or looking at her face. For the first time, I was really seeing the woman she has become.

I noticed the fact that she speaks with her eyes, just like me and her smile lights up a room. I paid attention to how clearly she articulates her thoughts and feelings, with sincerity, honesty and conviction. She exudes confidence and strength. Her voice inflection and words breathe kindness and passion. I also saw the potential of the BEAST she'd involuntarily inherited from both her father and me. Although tamed by the power of awareness, still ever so present. I could go on and on, but my point is, I could see the strong foundation of a beautiful and intelligent young lady. Not a female dog, video vixen, or a THOT. On the contrary, my baby girl has become an exquisitely FLY young WOMAN!

I can already hear the voices out there, *"Well, why does she seem surprised???"* To be honest, I am sincerely grateful! In our current culture, being a *lady* has seemingly become obsolete! It seems to be some type of farce to this generation to carry yourself in a manner befitting of respect and honor. When I was growing up the caliber of women I had to look up to was vastly different from the examples our babies have now.

Let me clarify *my* perception of what a lady is so there is no confusion about what I mean. To me a lady is graceful and poised, elegant and classy. She is both compassionate and kind, yet strong and no nonsense. She carries herself with dignity and gives others the respect she expects to receive. She fears God and loves His people. She prays and serves home, church and community. She loves her family unconditionally and protects them by any means necessary. She is quiet and observant. When she enters the room, her very presence commands attention and shifts the atmosphere, before she even opens her mouth.

This description may sound like a fairy tale to some, but for me I see this woman vividly! I call this woman mommy, auntie, sister, cousin, teacher, and first lady. This example of a lady includes the women in my family to the teachers in my elementary school. Even the women I admired in entertainment like Phylicia Rashad, Cicely Tyson, Diahann Carroll, Lena Horne, Patti Labelle etc., were prime examples of what it was to be a lady. When I was growing up there were examples of women all around me as a reminder that being a lady is fly!

What do I mean by the term *fly*? When I use the word, I am referring to being cool, classy, amazing, wonderful, great and excellent. The women I mentioned were proof that you can be sexy, without being naked. Your presence speaks, before you say a word. You can be flirty, without being trashy. You can be soft without being a doormat. You can be sassy and stand for what you believe, without being rude and condescending. They taught me to know my worth, know who I am, and to never compromise my values and morals. They taught me to stand for something or I'll fall for anything. They taught me to be a forever student and continue learning life's lessons and then teach what I learn. They taught me to own my past with pride because every experience assists in creating the woman I am to become. They taught me self-love, self-care, self-acceptance and self-confidence. They taught me that the truth will always out live a lie and to hold my head up high, no matter what!

My message to all women, whoever you are, in all walks of life, it's still *fly* to be a *lady*! Carry yourselves in a manner that constantly and consistently exudes characteristics reflective of the woman within. Give those watching you a positive role model by displaying ladylike qualities. Teach them lessons they can pass on to the next generation. Cultivate your potential and hold yourself to a standard of excellence that demands dignity and respect. And most importantly, prove to this generation that being a *lady* is still absolutely, positively, unquestionably and undeniably.... *fly*!

Lesson Principles:

1. Being a lady is timeless.

2. You don't have to conform to the culture in order to get the best out of life.

3. Set a standard for yourself and be a good example for those watching you.

Let's Pray:

Lord, help us not to conform to the things of this world but to be transformed by the renewing of our minds. In Jesus' name. Amen.

LESSON 18:

"The Why Factor"

"What's your why? When you know why you do what you do even the toughest days become easier." (Anon)

Every New Year I notice an alarming number of us making the same old New Year's resolutions. You know the ones I'm talking about, like, *"I'm definitely going to eat better this year and exercise more."* Or *"I'm going to finally going to complete that project I started last year."* We make promises to start that journal, save money, invest in that business, take that trip, and/or pursue that new career. The list goes on and these are the promises we can all look forward to from others and even make them to ourselves. I'm certainly guilty! I would set all these goals, yet by the end of the year I had missed out on the trip, done nothing to prepare for that business and mysteriously wound up gaining even *more* baby fat!

Well, this year I sat down and decided to figure out what I was doing wrong. Why is it that I can set these personal goals, with the very best intentions in mind and heart, yet still fail to attain them? I felt as if I were failing myself. As I contemplated this question, the words of Starbucks owner Howard Schultz hit me like a 100-pound boulder, *"It's not WHAT you do, it's WHY you do it!"* And just like that, I had the antidote to every broken promise I made to myself, New Year's or otherwise. I had to be clear about the *why*.

You see, when we set personal goals with no reason, cause or purpose in mind, it registers to the brain that our sacrificing or potential suffering isn't worth the desired outcome. Our bodies are slaves to our minds, and overtime, our willpower breaks under the pressure of our fleshly desires. It becomes almost impossible for us to remain consistent, disciplined and focused on the mission at hand! However, if we could at our very weakest moments, remember the *why* we can overcome hurdles of difficulty in order to achieve our goals. *Why are* you working so hard to lose the weight? *Why* you're putting the extra money aside? *Why* do you want to pursue next level education? *Why* did you start the blog, vlog or ministry? Our motives are just as significant as the actual work we put into obtain the desired outcome!

Completing this book was an aspiration of mine for two years before it came to fruition. I began this project very sure about its purpose which is to utilize my life experiences to encourage, inspire and empower other purpose driven women to live successfully in every area of their lives. It only took me about nine months to finish the lessons and put it in the hands of an editor. This chic ripped me to shreds! I wasn't prepared for the feedback I received, nor was I strong enough as a writer to take her words as constructive criticism and press forward to create a great piece of work. At that time, it was just easier for me to bury the entire project.

A year later I was sitting at the book release of one of my former clients. She said to me, *"I want to thank you for encouraging me to pursue all that God has placed within me and for pushing me to my purpose. I thank God for you."* In that instant, I was reminded of the *why factor*. Her words breathed life back into my mission and vision. She'd reminded me of the very reason I started this journey to begin with. At that moment, I knew it was time for me to get back to work and complete this book.

My husband likes to refer to *the why factor* as the heartbeat of our intentions. And we all know what happens when the heart stops beating. If we just keep the *why* at the forefront of our minds, coupled with hard work and determination, consistency and persistence there is NOTHING we can't achieve! Before you know it, your previous goals have been met and you're in pursuit of something new!

Lesson Principles:

1. Set realistic goals.

2. Always remember the *why* associated with the task.

3. Know that God has already given you all that you need.

Let's Pray:

Father, in the name of Jesus, Your Word declares that He that has begun a good work in us shall perform it. I pray that You would help us not to just set goals for good works in our lives but remain focused on the why so that we will complete every task that You set before us. In Jesus' name. Amen.

LESSON 19:

"Love Your Future Self Enough"

"Do something today that your future self will thank you for." (Anon)

Dear Future Self,

There are a few things that I need you to know. First, I need you to know that I believe in you! I believe in every dream you will ever dream, and I know that you have the power and ability to make them come true. Know that you are smart and strong, witty, vivacious, and charismatic. You are beautiful both inside and out. You are graceful, poised, well spoken, and intelligent. You possess a magnetic energy that fills any room you enter. Your smile exudes the joy and confidence that you carry within and your laugh is infectious! You have worked so hard and overcome so much to become the woman that you are today. NEVER compromise her for anything or anyone!

I need you to know the huge heart that God has given you is a blessing. At times, it may leave you susceptible to immense hurt. However, it will also allow you to love people purely and deeply as God has loved you. I need you to know that you have been given a natural ability to encourage, inspire, and empower those around you. God allows you to bring forth all that a person carries within and propel them to purpose. Because of this gift, you will attract different people with a variety of agendas and hidden motives. It is okay to protect yourself by creating personal boundaries. Realize to be close to you is a privilege that you cannot grant to just anyone. No matter how you feel at any given moment, you are never alone. God is always with you and He is strategic about the people He has connected to you.

No matter how much love and kindness you show those around you, some people will be offended that they are not a part of your inner circle. This is their issue, not yours! Do not bend or allow guilt to take a seat in your heart or mind. Your responsibility is to exercise wisdom and your innate ability to discern those around you. Recognize divine connections and weed out the rest, unapologetically.

Every decision I make, I do so with you in mind. I maintain my focus on you. I allow relationships to develop and/or dissolve with your best interest at heart. I study diligently and cultivate my potential in hopes that you live out your God given Purpose. I pray fervently for you. I fight every moment of every day so that you will be the woman you were created to be. I cry for you, hope for you, and ache for you. I love you and will continue to push past any obstacles to ensure that you become undeniably and unapologetically great!

I would encourage every woman to write a personal, heartfelt letter to the woman you're working to become. Speak candidly to her. Articulate what you're doing and the why behind it. Write down your goals, expectations and prayers. Once you've thoroughly communicated your thoughts, keep it before you. Read it out loud to yourself, often. Putting this into practice will keep you motivated and in full pursuit of the greatest version of yourself.

Lesson Principles:

1. Frequently remind yourself of the person you're striving to become.
2. Love on your future self, often.
3. Speak positivity, pray often and work hard, with the future in mind.

Let's Pray:

Lord, Your Word declares that You knew me before I was formed in my mother's womb. Before I was born You set me apart for a specific plan and purpose. Help me to believe Your word concerning me and help me to become that person and fulfill the purpose You have for me. In Jesus' name. Amen.

LESSON 20:

"Truth Heals"

"On the mountains of truth you can never climb in vain: either you will reach a point higher up today, or you will be training your powers so that you will be able to climb higher tomorrow."
(Friedrich Nietzsche)

Ever since I was a little girl, like many of you, I've heard the phrase "truth hurts." Without even realizing it, I adopted this statement as law because if everyone said it, it must be true. I began to study people's reaction to the truth. It seemed to validate the fact that pain was somehow connected to truth. For example, in church when someone was called out for their wrongs or sins, there would be one of two reactions. They would either weep from what seemed to be guilt or become flushed with feelings of shame and embarrassment. Then there were those moments in school when my classmates would exaggerate truths about one another, to intentionally direct negative attention to the other children. Saying things like "you have a big nose" or "look at her ears" and even complexion shaming for being too dark or too light. No matter what the "truth" was, I watched as the receiver, more times than not, had a negative response.

It wasn't until the morning of February 27th, 2016 that my perception fully shifted. I vividly recall sitting at my job having an intense conversation with a girlfriend. She decided to share with me a "truth" about myself. She said, "Tammy" (that's what they call me at work) "you're a dreamer and although I respect that, you're going to have to learn to plan for the things that you want." I could feel my breathing pattern begin to change. For me, this was a sign that her words were affecting me. (remember earlier I explained the importance of paying attention to my triggers, so I can control my response) She continued, "If you're going to have big dreams, you've got to have a great plan in place to execute them. You can't have a champagne dream, on a beer budget. SLOW DOWN! Everything you want will manifest in time, but you have got to SLOW DOWN. I don't ever want to see you hurt like this again." Hearing this harsh truth, on this day, from this friend immediately sent me into a whirlwind of different emotions. The most noticeable was shame. Even with that, I knew this was a God moment. I knew if I handled this correctly, I could walk away with yet another piece to this puzzle called life. The choice was mine; I chose to listen.

You're probably wondering what she could have possibly been referring to?! Some of you may be asking yourselves if my girlfriend was just jealous or perhaps a dream killer. On the contrary, she was a true friend. You see this conversation came exactly six months after the failure of me and my husband's grand vow renewal. Being the organizer that I am, I planned it for over a year and had everything in place. Just five months before our nuptials, without warning, I was sued for a ten-year old unpaid debt from my previous marriage. My wages were garnished. I was too embarrassed to say anything and had too much pride to ask for help. I fought to get my money back and filed documentation to cease the garnishment, but the paperwork wasn't processed in time. I just kept working overtime, planning and literally praying for a miracle. For me, this became an act of faith.

The morning of our vow renewal everything fell apart. To say that I was devastated is an understatement! Instead of making calls, we sent out mass texts to tell over 100 people our event had been cancelled. Our phones rang off the hook, but the embarrassment wouldn't allow me to talk to anyone. I quickly fell into a deep depression. The only thing that saved me was unconditional love of my husband and our confidants.

Having this conversation with my friend almost felt like an out of body experience. I was forced to relive one of the most difficult times of my life. Yet, I could feel God close to me, holding me in place. I felt the sincerity in her voice through every word spoken. I knew she loved me and her only desire was to see me become the very best version of myself. She needed to see me grow and longed to aide in my process in any way that she could. It was that very moment that I grasped the facts about truth. During that conversation I learned, truth heals! In that moment, completely submerged in truth, I instantly received complete healing!

Through my very own personal experiences I realized *truth* has been getting a bad rep. It is not the honesty itself that causes hurt or healing, but how it is internalized by the receiver. When delivered with malicious intent or if you just aren't ready, truth can be perceived as painful. Yet, when spoken with kindness and compassion, it brings about the possibility of the individual becoming healthy and whole. It opens the door for cleansing and restoration. Speak truth in sincerity and love. Accept truth in gratitude and hope for a greater future.

Lesson Principles:

1. Know that truth comes from God.

2. Speak truth in love.

3. Receive truth with hope.

Let's Pray:

Father, in the name of Jesus, Your Word says in John 8:32, "...and you will know the truth, and the truth will set you free." God help us to speak and receive Your truth in love, so that we, Your people, will no longer be bound by the lies of the enemy rather liberated by Your Word. In Jesus' name. Amen.

LESSON 21:

"You Train People How to Treat You"

"What you allow is what will continue."
(unknown)

For the most part I've gone into each relationship, both friendships and romance, with a positive outlook and an open mind. At a young age I adopted the golden rule, "Treat people how you want to be treated." As a result, of course I expected the same in return. However, as we live and learn we discover this isn't always how situations unfold. Just because you give people your best doesn't necessarily mean you're going to get theirs in return.

Due to this truth, building strong relationships became a little complicated for me. At the first sight of discord or tension, I was out! This was for two reasons. One, I had very high expectations for the people that I allowed into my space, which weren't very many. When they didn't meet those expectations, I would take that as a sign that they would eventually hurt me and didn't deserve the opportunity to be in my life, in any capacity. Of course, this mentality didn't develop overnight. It became a defense mechanism after being hurt by friends that I held dear as well as family members.

I can recall a time that I opened a cell phone account for my *best friend.* She had just moved back to Miami from

Georgia and needed a little help getting her bearings. She was offered a teaching position and already had a place to stay. So, when she asked, there was no hesitation! Besides, all she must do was keep the bill current, which was maybe $50 a month at the time. There was no long drawn out conversation. No contract written up and signed between us. We had years of friendship and trust built between us. She had the means to handle it. The rest, to me, was good sense and common courtesy. What could go wrong?!

Not only did she NOT keep up with the bill, but she added two additional lines to the account AND allowed them all to become delinquent. I didn't find all of this out until I went to open an account for my children as Christmas gift and I was given a balance owed of almost $500. Instantly, I felt a warm rush of blood fill my head. I was LIVID! Which leads me to the second reason I am hesitant when connecting with people; my temper. I felt betrayed, swindled, and ultimately plain old tried. This can take me from 0 to 100 quickly. I was newly saved at the time and I loved God with all my heart. Yet, I could imagine myself wrapping my hands around her neck, on sight! To avoid that whole scenario, I chalked it up to a loss and washed my hands of the relationship. My husband, who was my boyfriend at the time, paid the bill for me and I moved on with my life. I also made a promise to myself to never let it happen again.

After a few isolated years, I started to over analyze myself. *"Is something wrong with me?"* *"Am I pushing good people away?"* *"Maybe I just like being alone."* *"Maybe my personality is too abrasive?"* I finally decided to talk to my best friend: my husband. I was like, "Baby, am I a nice person?" In true Bobbo fashion he responded, "I mean, you're nice to who you're nice to." That didn't help at all. He then asked me what was on my mind. I shared with him my thoughts of friendship, how I handle them and why. With wisdom beyond his years he looked at me and said, "You train people how to treat you by what you accept. That's not fair to you or them." I tried to plead my case by telling him I hate when people do things that I would never do to them. He said, "Shawn, you train people how to treat you with what you accept. If it's something you don't like or won't tolerate, tell them!" This conversation helped me realize I was filtering new relationships through my past hurts and potentially missing out on some great connections and even life-long friendships.

Almost immediately my perception of the people I choose to connect with shifted. This included my friendships, family relationships, business partnerships, coworkers, clients, church members and even my marriage. If something is said or done that concerns or offends you, don't automatically assume it was done intentionally. Communicate your thoughts and feelings before you distance yourself. Most important, be upfront and open about your expectations with the people entering your circle of trust. Although applying these principles doesn't change the past, they have certainly helped me to establish long lasting friendships and increase my level of trust and vulnerability with those around me.

None of us are perfect so we should give people the benefit of the doubt. This isn't to say offense or disrespect won't happen though that is the hope. You must teach the people around you what you will and will not tolerate. Subsequently, if and when people are removed from your inner circle, both parties are very clear on the reason(s) why.

Lesson Principles:

1. Be very clear about your expectations of the people in your life.

2. Don't expect perfection from people, when you yourself are not perfect.

3. Show people the same patience and love that you want to be shown.

Let's Pray:

Father, in the name of Jesus, I know that You have specific people assigned to my life. People that will teach me, stretch me and help me grow. Reveal these people to me and teach me how to show people the same grace and mercy that You have so mercifully shown towards me. In Jesus' name. Amen.

LESSON 22:

"Not Everyone Can Handle All of You"

*"Be who you are and say what you feel,
because those who mind don't matter,
and those who matter don't mind."
(Bernard M. Baruch)*

As children, most of us were taught to put our best foot forward, at all times. There are even cute little phrases and quotes validating this fact. Sayings such as, "The first impression is a lasting impression." or, "You only get one chance to make a first impression" emphasize the weight we put into the way others perceive us. For that reason, we wear our brightest smiles, engage in conversation attentively and with charisma even when we don't really want to. All of this in an effort to give the best of who we are when meeting new people.

While there are benefits to putting your best at the forefront, there are also some drawbacks. People begin to expect the same energy and demeanor you initially present. They expect this side of you on a regular basis. This expectation can have one of two effects. One, you can put grave pressure on yourself to portray the image that you know people require of you, no matter how you feel. Two, you can realize that no one is perfect, and everyone deserves the right to have an off-day sometimes. This shouldn't be considered fake, phony or a disappointment to those around you, it is simply part of our human nature.

Becoming the wife of a pastor was one of the most difficult challenges I've faced to date. I learned very quickly that people had very high expectations of me. I had inadvertently become a picture of hope and example of Christianity to the young women within my sphere of influence. This wasn't just within the walls of the building but everywhere I went. Women I worked with, women at the salon, in the grocery store, even those on social media put me under a microscope. People set a standard for me that I wasn't privy to. Unfortunately, I was not yet equipped, nor was I ready to live up to their guidelines. Either way, my new position and their suppositions of me were here to stay.

I was a novice, so I attempted to please everyone. I hid my flaws and failures as best I could, for the sake of not being prejudged or causing another woman to stumble. I attempted to portray the picture of perfection I felt they needed me to emulate. I didn't know how to create boundaries. I wasn't sure who to trust and who to keep at bay. I would feel a certain way about things going on in the church but stayed quiet as not to offend anyone. I was not being my authentic self. Overtime, my life as a First Lady became an implosion just waiting to happen.

I succumbed to the worst-case scenario. My imperfections disappointed someone in the church. She didn't like the way I handled the dismantling of a woman's group. She felt she should have had input. The young lady was so upset, she left the ministry. In my mind, it was solely because of me. Despite all the adjustments I made, my worst fears still came true. In my eyes, my actions caused someone to leave the church. I cried and moped around for months. My husband finally came to me and said, "You did the best you could, and your intentions were pure. You will not allow this or anything else to break you. We will learn from it, pray the best for those that are gone and move forward." That was the last day I cried about that incident.

My words to you are: life is a process. You will make mistakes and disappoint some people in the process, but don't fret. You will be better, stronger and wiser because of it. You are constantly going to learn, grow, stretch and evolve. There are some that will love you for it. Yet, not everyone will appreciate you, some are not equipped to handle, nor deserve the *you* that will be revealed overtime. Come to grips with the actuality that not everyone is supposed to be close to you. The sooner you accept that, the more at peace you will be.

Lesson Principles:

1. No one is perfect! Never put on a front to please someone else.

2. Don't allow yourself to be held captive by the expectations of imperfect people.

3. Know that there are people that will love you for exactly who you are.

Let's Pray:

Father, in the name of Jesus, I thank You that Your Word says in Psalms 139:14, "I am fearfully and wonderfully made." God, I pray that You help me to live in the truth of what You say about me and I pray the God connections that You have ordained for me will unfold in my life. In Jesus' name. Amen.

Lesson 23:

"An Apology Isn't Always Enough"

"Forgiveness is the best form of love. It takes a strong person to say sorry and an even stronger person to forgive."
(Unknown)

I'm the one that will apologize at the drop of a dime. Once I realize I am the cause of the hurt or harm of someone I care about I am immediately willing to apologize. There have been times when I don't even know that I'm entirely wrong in a situation, but for the sake of the relationship I will apologize so we can move past the issue. I also expected my apology to be accepted immediately. I mean, the whole purpose of saying *I'm sorry* is so we can move forward. If I'm accepting responsibility, what more is in question?

Well, for some people, *"I'm sorry"* are just mere words. These words just aren't enough. My husband is one of those people. For him, the verbal apology is just the beginning of the process. My perception was different, therefore I had a difficult time adjusting to his method of handling an apology. In my mind his approach kept us at odds, while mine afforded us the opportunity to squash the issue and get back to normal. To me, he was wrong and I was right, which ultimately created a deeper issue.

Since we're both stubborn, this became a battle. Overtime I adopted the philosophy, *"If you can't beat them join them"* and I stopped apologizing. This created a recipe for disaster in our marriage. Now anytime there was a disagreement we would just walk around with tension, not speaking at all. That quiet time in anger was a breeding ground to formulate negative thoughts. Once we did start talking, we had gotten so far away from the original issue that the argument started all over again.

One day we were having a candid conversation about effective ways to communicate. I asked him why it seemed as if he still had an issue, even after I apologize. He told me it wasn't that he didn't accept my apology, but for him that doesn't instantaneously make everything better. I must be honest and say that, at first, I was confused. For me an apology translated into everything being okay, now let's move on. For him it meant the person just wants to skip past the issue instead of handling it, so it doesn't happen again. While we had to respect one another's differences of opinion, we still needed come up with a compromise that worked for us both. While we both agree that apologies are important, now we also view them as a segue into a conversation about whatever the initial issue was and how we can prevent it from occurring again.

Although apologies are a very necessary part of any

healthy relationship, they may translate into something very different for everyone. While this may not be a popular topic of discussion, me and my husband realized it is important to express to your partner and close friends how *you* process apologies. Most of us apologize to assume responsibility for a wrong and commit to change. However, the acceptance of that apology is left entirely up to the offended party. It is extremely important to be receptive to one's offering of remorse, especially if you want to move past the offense and avoid a future breakdown of communication in the relationship. Nevertheless, you DO NOT get to dictate if and/or when acceptance is accepted. Nor do you get a say on whether they let you back into their space in the same capacity as before! That is the risk we take when we hurt the people we say we love.

Lesson Principle:

1. Apologize with no expectations of the offended person.

2. Be patient with people that you know you have hurt.

3. Hold yourself accountable for the things you say and do to avoid having to be apologetic.

Let's Pray:

Proverbs 10:12 says, "Hatred stirs up strife, but love covers all offenses." Lord, help me to lead with love in all that I say and do. In Jesus' name. Amen.

LESSON 24:

"True Friendship Takes Time"

"Friendship, not unlike Love, takes time. Don't rush it!" (LaShawn Spry)

I love people! It's how God made me. I have always been bubbly, personable and open to everyone. The method I used with the people in my life was not unlike the method my 10th grade English teacher, Ms. Ray, used with her students. She stood in front of the class on the first day of school and explained to us her grading system. Ms. Ray said we all would start out with an "A" in her class, whether we maintained that grade or not, was entirely up to us. Maintaining a high average was predicated on a combination of different tasks: how much we studied, our test scores, and the overall amount of work we put into the class were all considered.

The same held true for me with the people I allowed into my life. I would start everyone off with an "A" and it was their job to maintain that high mark. In my mind, it wasn't a difficult task. As long as you put in the work to get to know me, be there for me when I need you, communicate with me, tell the truth, be the same behind my back that you are to my face, remain loyal and defend me if and when necessary, then you will always have a high grade in my book!

The problem with my system of choice was that

unlike Ms. Ray, I never communicated the rules of engagement to the other party. Yet, if they violated, I would create immediate distance, no questions asked, nor explanation given. I rationalized these actions with my own personal logic. I would say to myself, "They should have known better." or "I would have never done that to them." This mindset is dangerous because it makes you act as if you're the perfect friend and everyone else is flawed.

Though my intentions were good, I had to learn a better, more productive way to handle the relationships in my life. That's when I embraced the value of taking my time getting to know people for who they are and vice versa. I learned to be kind and cordial with everyone, yet cautious about those I allow to occupy my intimate space; the place specifically designated for divine connections. Divine connections are those people strategically assigned to your life. The ones that will assist you in discovering, pursuing, and ultimately fulfilling your God given purpose.

When it comes to friendship, long term or short term, time is your greatest ally. It exposes true character and integrity and creates a solid foundation of endurance and strength. Time reveals weaknesses and imperfections, while affording you the opportunity to break down and rebuild, if you so choose to. When you move slowly in relationship building, it forces you to be patient and avoid making unnecessary mistakes that carry long term consequences. From this moment forward, pray that God will expose the heart and intentions of those that attempt to connect with you. Then allow time to do its perfect work and create forever friendships with the people God sends into your life.

Lesson Principles:

1. Take your time when building relationships.

2. Listen more than you speak. Pay attention to what people are showing you about themselves.

3. Be kind to everyone, but only allow a few into your intimate space.

Let's Pray:

Father in the name of Jesus, I pray that You would open the eyes of my heart so that I can see people for exactly who they are. God, I pray that you would reveal to me those connections that You have ordained for my life. Help me to nurture, value and cultivate them so that they blossom into whatever You have designed them to be. I pray that any ties that have been created that are not in my best interest be exposed and severed. In Jesus' name I pray. Amen.

LESSON 25:

"Cherish Life's Jewels; You're Only Gifted a Few"

"Forever friends are a treasure chest of understanding and compassion. Cherish them." (Amy Leigh Mercree)

Bishop T.D. Jakes penned a sermon called "Three Types of People in Your Life." In this sermon he places people into three different categories; comrades, confidants, and constituents. While all three of these groups of people are very much necessary, they are not all permanent fixtures in your life. Your *constituents* are *for* what you are for. *Comrades* are against what you are against. But your *confidants* are those people that are for you. These are the people in your life that love you unconditionally. They don't care about your money, your weight, your looks or lifestyle. These are your soulmate friends that will love you for the long haul. These are the people that you share your dreams with. They will respect, support and encourage your dreams and visions because they love you. Bishop T.D. Jakes says, "If you get two or three of these in a lifetime, you are a blessed individual."

These confidants are the people I have pegged as my *Jewels*. I didn't discover my *Jewels* until later in life. Not because they weren't there but because I wasn't equipped to nurture and value these relationships. You can only be blessed with these types of friendships after you've learned to *be* this kind of friend. Since I was raised alone and independent, I felt I could manage life alone. I was under the misconception that I didn't need anyone for support or encouragement; I could make it by myself. Besides, people only want to be close to you to find out your business, then either spread it to others or make themselves feel better about their own mess. Over the years I became guarded and extremely selfish with my space and time. I would let people in only as much as I deemed comfortable and safe.

It wasn't until 2008, when I decided to dedicate my life to Christ that I realized the value of life's jewels. The more I learned about Jesus Christ and embraced His unconditional love for me, the more selfless and vulnerable I became. I wanted to extend the love I felt to others but there was no one around. I was in a different season in my life, therefore, the people around me had to change. The people I went to the club with, drank with, stayed out all night and partied with had fallen away. For a while I found myself in a very lonely space. I began to wonder where my *true* friends were.

It was during this time of my life that I sought out my *Jewels*. These are the people around me that encourage me and pray fervently for me, love me unconditionally and are honest with me, even when the truth stings. My circle protects my dreams and visions and pushes me to pursue my purpose. The faithful few that always defend me behind my back, celebrate me to my face, invest in me and want to see me win. Most importantly, my jewels allow me to do the exact same for each of them!

God never intended for us, His children, to travel life's journey alone. He intentionally connects us with a specific group of people that will help us to develop into the person He predestined us to be. It is His will that we encourage one another, help one another and love one another. God blesses us for the sole purpose of us being a blessing to one another not just financially, but also with support, encouragement and unconditional love.

All of us have been blessed with life's *Jewels*. Those people that God has specifically assigned to your life to be your cheerleaders, your team and ultimately help you win! Ask God to reveal them to you and when He does, cherish them because they are vital to your success as you are.

Lesson Principles:

1. Know the difference between your comrades, constituents, and confidants.
2. Ask God to reveal the people He has assigned to your life.
3. Be the type of friend to others that you want them to be to you.

Let's Pray:

Father, in the name of Jesus, I realize that You have placed us on this Earth not to be selfish, but to be a blessing to one another. I pray that You will help me use the resources that You have blessed me with to be a blessing to those around me. Increase my gift of discernment to recognize the difference between my constituents, comrades, and confidants. And help to love all people, You love me. In Jesus' name. Amen.

LESSON 26:

"Let Your Light Shine"

"Never dim your light so the insecurities of others can be comfortably concealed."
(LaShawn Spry)

How often do you dim your light because you care too much about what others think? Have you ever minimized your shine for fear of how others may feel or what others may say? Do you take the judgement of others into consideration when making decisions? How many times have you downplayed the very attributes and characteristics that make you unique, for the sake of making someone else feel more comfortable in their own pool of self-doubt and insecurity. If you're anything like me, it's probably been more times than you can recall.

My personality is a light. My smile is a light. My laughter is a light. My voice is a light. My style is a light. My boldness is a light. My genuineness is a light. My love is a light. Everything that makes me authentically who I am is also what makes me shine so bright in this world. My very presence speaks volumes. I don't say this to be braggadocios, I am sharing my truth. For this reason, many are drawn to me, while others reject me. I have such a great love for people that once I noticed there were things about me that made people shrink, I begin to dull my personality for their comfort.

Over time I could see that I was not only stifling my

own growth and success, but also doing the other person a disservice. The Bible says that we are to be *"the salt and the light of the World."* God has already shown me that it is my responsibility to encourage, inspire and empower others to live every area of lives purposefully and successfully. If I am not exuding purpose and success, then what good am I to the people in my sphere of influence? By boldly and confidently being the woman God created me to be, He can use my light to shine a light of hope in the lives of other women. God can push them out of the illusions and lies of darkness, into His marvelous light.

It is your duty to let your light shine bright! Don't settle for someone else's comfort with stagnation and complacency. Your desire and passion are greater than such small mindedness. Being certain about who God made you doesn't make you cocky or arrogant. You don't have to walk around being constrained by timidity. Be your most genuine self always, no matter who feels uncomfortable. This will either inspire or intimidate; neither of which is your concern. Ultimately, that choice is not about you. People will receive you based on where they currently are in their lives. Embrace those who flourish in your light and pray for those that do not.

I would like to close this lesson with a beautiful quote by Marianne Williamson:

> *"Our deepest fear is not that we are inadequate. Our deepest fear is that we are powerful beyond measure. It is our light, not our darkness that most frightens us. We ask ourselves, who am I to be brilliant, gorgeous, talented, fabulous? Actually, who are you not to be? You are a child of God. Your playing small does not serve the world. There is nothing enlightened about shrinking so that other people won't feel insecure around you. We are all meant to shine, as children do. We were born to make manifest the glory of God that is within us. It's not just in some of us; it's in everyone. And as we let our own light shine, we unconsciously give other people permission to do the same. As we are liberated from our own fear, our presence automatically liberates others."*

How beautiful would this world be, if we all gave ourselves permission to let our God given light shine, in turn granting others the same consent? Shine bright purposeful people!

Lesson Principles:

1. Your light is a gift from God that makes you special.

2. Always be the most authentic version of yourself.

3. Their comfort is not your responsibility.

Let' Pray:

God, Your Word calls for us to be the salt and the light of the World. Help us to shine brightly in such a way that we ignite change in the hearts and minds of Your people and inspire others to seek You wholeheartedly. In Jesus' name we pray. Amen.

Lesson 27:

"Remain Unbothered by the Opinions of People"

"We do ourselves a great disservice when we let the opinions of others mingle and subvert our own thoughts." (Dodinsky)

Opinionated know-it-alls are my absolute favorite people!!! (said no one ever) These individuals had become the bane of my existence. I am sure it is for that very reason that I became a magnet for them. Their judgments, thoughts and feelings on how everyone, including me, could live so much better by simply following their unsolicited advice, drove me absolutely insane!

I was fortunate enough (or unfortunate depending on your perception) to have an immediate family member that always had an opinion about other people's lives. So, I grew a disdain for this personality type at a very young age. That character trait, coupled with her strong opinions were just enough to rub those that encountered her the wrong way. The sad part is, I don't believe she even realized how much her blunt point of view turned people off. The older I became the more I realized that this was really her attempt to help. Most times, unfortunately, that genuine desire to help was eclipsed by the brash delivery.

The tension with this particular family member all came to a head in the worst possible way. My elderly mother was rushed to the hospital and needed to have open heart surgery, which left my bedridden father who suffers from dementia without a caretaker. For this reason, among others, a family meeting was called.

I always dreaded these gatherings. Since I was the youngest, I didn't the bond with my siblings that they had with one another. I would usually remain quiet and just go with the flow of whatever decisions they decided to make. However, this time was different. When asked, I decided to speak up regarding the matter at hand. And when I did share what I felt would be the best option, the response I received was, "That's just your immaturity speaking." In that moment, all the feelings that I suppressed from the past, of being dismissed or brushed off by my siblings came rushing back into my mind. Over thirty years of built up frustration came spewing out of my mouth through words and a tone that to this day still haunt me. I allowed my emotions to get the best of me. In my mind, this person's perception of me would never change. To them I was always going to be the younger, less successful, less educated sister that didn't make the life choices she thought I should make.

I beat myself up for quite some time after this incident, wishing over and over that I could take it all back.

That is until I realized, this was yet another teaching moment for me. Standing up to my sister that day revealed that I overvalue her opinion of me and undervalue my own. I viewed her as my role model and up to that point I spent my life seeking her validation. That moment forced me to stop holding myself to her standards; to stop allowing myself to feel inferior. This confrontation, though uncomfortable, gave me the clarity to perceive myself through the lens of God. I gained the courage to hold onto what I know to be true and not become emotionally bothered by the perceptions of others, no matter who they are.

The reality is that every single person on this Earth has an opinion about everything and everyone; including you and me! We filter people and situations through the lens of our own personal experiences, beliefs, morals, standards, and values. The way we were raised, our family dynamic, financial status, relationships, level of education, and religious beliefs all play a role in the way we make assessments. Whether you find yourself facing the judgment of a loved one as in the case of me and my sister or sitting at a round table full of business executives, we cannot permit the opinions or point of view of others to penetrate our minds and hearts to such a degree that our emotions are rattled. On the contrary, our only responsibility is to listen openly, extend respect to one another while simultaneously standing on the cusps of and confidently speaking what we know to be our truth.

Lesson Principles:

1. Everyone is entitled to their own opinion.
2. You don't have to accept someone else's view as your truth.
3. Listen to others respectfully and speak your truth in love.

Let's Pray:

Lord, help me to know my truth and give me the courage to stand unwaveringly, unapologetically and unbothered by different perspectives and perceptions of others. In Jesus' name. Amen.

Lesson 28:

"Healed People, Heal People"

"Other people are going to find healing in your wounds. Your greatest life messages and your most effective ministry will come out of your deepest hurts." (Rick Warren)

Growing up I would hear my mom use a phrase something like this, *"The blind leading the blind and they all gone fall in a ditch."* As a child the quote was somewhat humorous to me. My thought of course was, "Why would a blind person even attempt to lead someone else?" As I matured I realized the statement was a metaphor used to accurately describe a common scenario that occurs in real life. People try to give instruction and advice on life situations and circumstances that they know nothing about. And because the poor, unsuspecting soul listening to the amateur is clueless and simply desperate for some immediate relief or change, they are usually willing to try anything. Hence, the blind leading the blind!

At one point the blind person attempting to lead, was me. I had been a First Lady for about a year and a half. I realized almost immediately my purpose was connected to women. My desire to see women spiritually, mentally and emotionally whole had become a passion that I could not ignore. I was eager to explore this new found desire. I prayed about it and then I went to my husband for some pastoral advice. I told him that I had been talking to God about it and asked him what he thought. As always, he supported me 100% with whatever vision God gave me. Yet, because he knows me so well, he sternly urged me to stay before God. The thing is, once my wheels get to turning I usually move impulsively without hesitation. My husband just wanted me to be sure I was not only well prepared for the assignment, but also that I was operating in God's perfect timing.

Not long after this conversation, in true *LaShawn* fashion, I planned my first event and it actually exceeded my expectations. Almost 30 women showed up willing to be transparent with their stories and open to receive nuggets of wisdom. These women yearned to be complete and whole. Unfortunately, I was the only person in the room whose story and feelings were still safely tucked away. The room was decorated with beautiful bright colors and the refreshments table was perfect. Without even realizing it, I'd placed my *mask* on just before we got started. I could safely teach, without appearing that I needed to be taught. I could publicly give, without receiving anything. I resolved in my mind that these women wouldn't listen to me if I didn't have it all together. I certainly couldn't share my brokenness with the very women I'm supposed to be helping. Is it that I can't or I'm just not ready yet? Was that not the very thing I was encouraging and asking of them? I know now this was totally oxymoronic and could not work.

Exactly one year later, almost to the day of our first meeting, this group of women was almost unrecognizable. Confusion and discord set in to the point that the group divided literally in two. I tried to salvage it through individual conversations with each member and even confronting issues in our group sessions, but nothing seemed to work. Since this no longer resembled the vision that God initially gave me, without warning, I completely dismantled the entire organization.

When I walked away from these women not only was I questioning my purpose, but I doubted if I'd heard God at all. I wondered, what happened? Why would God put me in this position and seemingly set me up to fail? It's so easy for us to immediately blame God instead of analyzing our own actions. I was confused and hurt. The pity party was in full affect, but I couldn't let these women see me sweat. So, instead of taking time to acknowledge the pain and learn from my mistakes, I did what I was used to doing and kept it moving. I threw myself into a whole new project!

This too fell apart. This time when it didn't work, my heart was shattered. I never gave myself a moment to grieve the loss of the first vision, I certainly wasn't strong enough to handle another blow so soon. My spirit was broken. But this time instead of ignoring my feelings, I faced them head on. I spent much needed time in prayer. Not so much talking, but listening for God's voice; waiting for His direction. He finally said, *"Shawn you're doing this all wrong. You're trying to help and heal everyone around you, without working on and revealing your own brokenness."* I was encouraging women to be open, but wasn't practicing the same vulnerability. I was attempting to lead blind women, while voluntarily remaining blind myself. I must have cried for a week straight; not just for me, but the women that depended on me. Despite my ignorance, God still moved in their lives.

What I couldn't see at the time was that God, in His infinite wisdom, replaced the deception of perfection with admitted brokenness. I became marred clay in the gentle hands of the Potter. He took the time to mold and shape me into the masterpiece He always knew I would be. Over time, the truth of God's Word healed my brokenness and straightened every crook in my life. Now that I have been through the healing process myself, I am equipped to effectively help other women heal.

There is someone waiting for the truth and transparency of your story. They are desperate for the healing and hope that your testimony will bring to their lives. Don't wait any longer. Give God all the burdens from your past, in exchange for the peace that He promised. Then, it becomes your duty to help someone else find that same healing through Christ Jesus.

Lesson Principles:

1. You cannot help someone when you are still bound.

2. Do not allow guilt and shame to hold you hostage to your past.

3. Complete healing comes through cultivating your relationship with God.

Let's Pray:

God, I thank You for the confirmation in Your Word that reminds us by Your stripes, we are healed. Help us to declare Your healing every day, in every area of our lives. In Jesus' name. Amen.

LESSON 29:

"Let Pride Die"

"They that know God will be humble; they that know themselves cannot be proud." (John Flavel)

For many years I was under the misconception that pride was a healthy characteristic to possess. I believed you should feel proud of your own personal accomplishments and successes. You owe it to yourself to applaud the wins and celebrate any progress you make, especially in those strenuous areas of life. I thought that pride was the fuel that ignited the fire which would catapult me into the future I'd always imagined for myself. For me, pride wasn't about me looking down on other people. It was about me lifting myself up. The ultimate problem with self-elevation is everything that goes up, eventually, must all come down. Proverbs 11:2 says it like this, *"When pride comes, then comes disgrace."* This Bible verse is proof that the fall of the proud is guaranteed.

The very definition of pride is a feeling or deep pleasure or satisfaction derived from one's own achievements, the achievements of those with whom one is closely associated, or from qualities or possessions that are widely admired. It is an emotion that often offends others, while implicating an inflated sense of self-worth or status. Pride can make you feel a sense of superiority over others. If you're not careful, you can easily come across as egotistical or arrogant.

This describes exactly how I felt while planning our vow renewal in 2015. Our relationship had been under scrutiny from day one, for various reasons. Since both of us failed at marriage previously, there were many people that felt we were rushing into this. And they certainly weren't afraid to voice their unsolicited opinions. When my husband and I planted the church, those closest to us didn't agree with our decision then either. Some called us reckless and asked if we were sure we heard God clearly. There were even family members that told us we should have come to them first, so they could seek God on our behalf. Because we obviously don't know the voice of God for ourselves, right?!

From previous lessons, you already know we started having financial challenges almost immediately after starting the church. The same people that talked about us and ridiculed our choices were the exact people we had to ask for help when things became difficult. It was not only embarrassing, it made me extremely angry; not just with them, but with God. I didn't understand why He would put us in a position where we would need people that didn't believe in us, nor did they support our choice to follow Him!

Needless to say, this wedding became the ultimate payback. The perfect opportunity to annihilate any derogatory opinions of our marriage and ministry in one-full-swoop. It was a way to let pessimists and advocates alike know the Sprys were doing just fine. I couldn't see it then, but my heart was filled with pride. So much so, that even when I realized we were in financial trouble due to my wage garnishment, I didn't say a word to anyone. And I made my husband promise to do the same. I refused to voluntarily give these people one more reason to scrutinize a choice we had made. Pride wouldn't let me see that by *not* saying anything privately, I was setting us up for a huge public failure.

Out of desperation, I tried to force God's hand. I prayed, I fasted, I cried, and I begged. I told God, *"I know You can turn this around and I'm trusting You to do it."* This was a true statement; my faith was strong and I just knew our obedience to Him had to count for something. We had been faithful in ministry even after losing our cars, home going into foreclosure, having to financially carry the church and home, people coming and going. We must have earned some type of cool points with God through all of this! The night before the wedding I went to the facility and prayed in the parking lot. I could clearly feel God guiding us to ask for help, but pride *still* would not let me. After the dust cleared, the worst part wasn't even the embarrassment, it was realizing how much our lack of transparency and honesty hurt those that genuinely love and want the best of us.

The Bible clearly states that God hates pride. He even warns us against embracing the haughty trait. It was never my place to prove a point or set people straight about their perception of my husband and me. I was to accept and live out God's will for our lives. I had to become conscious of the fact that being completely engulfed in self and what people think or say was not only detrimental to my spiritual and mental wellbeing, but also negatively affected those who truly love me. In Matthew 23:12 Jesus says, "Those who exalt themselves will be humbled, and those who humble themselves will be exalted." I don't know about you, but I would hate for God to ever have to humble me again. I learned through this fiasco, to humble myself.

Humility is the exact opposite of pride. It is

described as having a feeling of insignificance, inferiority, and subservience. Truthfully the more we learn about God, who He is in our lives and what He has done for us the more we realize we are NOTHING without Him. Once we come to this realization, it becomes much easier it is to *"Humble yourselves, therefore, under the mighty hand of God so that at the proper time He may exalt you."* (1 Peter 5:6)

Choosing humility over pride does not mean you cannot celebrate the wins and success along the way. God wants His very best for each of us. However, it *is* about recognizing the true source of all that is good in our lives James 1:12 says, *"Every good and perfect gift is from above."* It's about pointing every person in our territory back to God. Also, knowing without the shadow of a doubt, that we are absolutely nothing without Him.

Lesson Principles:

1. Make the conscious choice to remain humble.

2. Choosing pride sets you up for immense failure.

3. Realize God is the source of everything good.

Let's Pray:

Father God, You said in Your Word that pride comes before a disgrace. God we never want to bring shame to You or ourselves. Help us to remain humble in our hearts and minds and fully accept Your will, knowing that we are nothing without You. We will live in a posture of gratitude for what You have already done and all that You will do. In Jesus' name. Amen.

LESSON 30:

"There is a Process to Greatness"

"It is a rough road that leads to the heights of greatness." (Lucius Annaeus Seneca)

Marrying my husband was one of the greatest life changes I ever experienced. To understand the magnitude of that statement, you must understand the path that led me to him. By the time I meant Bobbo, I'd been engaged on several occasions and already failed miserably at marriage...TWICE!!! (yes, twice) I really don't even like to count the second time because it only lasted six months, but for the sake of this book, I'LL OWN IT!! It's safe to say, up to that point I had been unsuccessful at love. Yet, I still carried a glimmer of hope within that someday my forever love would find me. And by the grace of God, he did!

It sounds cliché, but we clicked immediately. We built a solid friendship and quickly fell in love. After only seven months he asked me to be his wife. I was overjoyed! Finally, God had allowed me to cross paths with the man that was going to love me just for me, for the rest of my life! A man that loves my children as his own. A man that respects and honors me and views me as an asset. A man that pushes me to be better and cultivates my God-given gifts and talents. The perfect depiction of my husband in my heart and mind is that Bobby is the representation of God's love for me in the Earth realm. A true follower of Christ, the head of our home, my best friend, my covering, my intercessor, my king, my love, my Bobbo.

We knew very early in our courtship that God had placed a great purpose on us individually and over our marriage. Given our past, we were both immensely grateful. I assumed that because our courting phase went so smoothly our marriage would follow suit. THE DEVIL LIED! The first few years of our marriage were simply HELL ON EARTH! No, seriously. Our very first argument came about, only a month into the marriage. We had moved into our new place together and I needed my things taken out of storage before the end of the month. I told Bobby and expected that he would handle it. Well, a week went by, and nothing. Two weeks went by, nothing. When I say nothing I mean no conversation about it, no questions, no update and no furniture. I then took it upon myself to give him what I thought was a friendly reminder.

Me: Baby don't forget my furniture has to be out by next Monday.

Him: You already told me that.

Me: Okay, I just wanted to make sure you hadn't forgotten because I don't want to lose my stuff.

Him: Baby, I don't forget anything you tell me.

Me: Okay, cool.

I felt a little bad and walked away scolding myself. "Shawn you know he isn't intense like you! He's not going to do things like you would." I said to myself, "Just chill and let him be the man. Don't be a nag!" That was Monday, seven days before my furniture had to be out.

Saturday, two days before the deadline, my furniture was still in storage. Again, there was no additional conversation, no more questions, certainly no update and NO FURNITURE. Now my eyebrows are raised. I'm saying to myself, "You said you don't forget, so do you just not care about my things?" I went downstairs into the kitchen for some water. He was into his usual routine for a Saturday in August, which was watching college football. Now I'm pissed and I have to say something! I walked in front of the television and the conversation went like this.

Me: You do know my storage unit expires Monday?

Him: Shawn I called my uncle, he hasn't answered me yet. I don't know anyone else with a truck and I'm not going to aggravate him. I've been working on it since you told me.

Me: Why didn't you just tell me that? I would've found someone myself, but I didn't want to step on your toes. I could've just handled it myself if I knew you were going to wait until the last minute! Now I could lose my stuff. (side note: *Ladies don't ever gloat about what you can accomplish without him! It's disrespectful and emasculating. It also makes him wonder what the heck he's there for! Back to the story.*)

Him: **continues watching TV and says nothing **

Me: **now feels like fire is shut up in my bones!! Wants to push the whole tv onto the floor, but instead I walk behind it and rip every chord out of the wall.**

Dude, you don't hear me talking to you? You just gone sit there and ignore me?

Then I had what I call a "red out". That's when I'm

so infuriated all I see is red and I can't even remember what was said or done. What I do know is my usually calm, laid back, soft spoken husband stood up from the couch and proclaimed,

Him: Don't worry about it, I'll leave. I swear I'll leave.

He then proceeded to walk up the stairs to the bedroom and close the door. I'm not exactly sure what was going through his mind at the time or my own mind for that matter. But one thing is certain, both of us walked away from that dark place wondering, "God, what in the world have I gotten myself into?!" The next day he and his uncle were moving all the furniture out of my storage unit and into the rental property. Although our house was now completely furnished, it was far from a home. That fight had spun us so far from our original state, that we didn't know how to get back. We decided it was best to go to counseling. One twinkle in time catapulted us into a two year recovery process. I had to learn to trust again, while my husband had to learn to forgive. It was hard work, but we always believed the purpose of our marriage was greater than its challenges. To this day when we are faced with adversity, we fight it together!

Fast forward ten years. There have been many disagreements, arguments, screaming matches, tears and more counseling sessions. There was also much prayer, determination, faith, forgiveness and at our core, friendship. Today we have a stronger, more solid marriage than we could have ever imagined. If we gave up when things became difficult, we would never have manifested the marriage that God predestined for us from the very beginning.

At the time we didn't understand that greatness requires a process that must be completed. A process that creates the solid foundation that is necessary to be able to stand the test of time. This process helped us develop trust, effective communication, unconditional love, intimacy, forgiveness and unbreakable friendship, in our marriage. Though our process was admittedly tedious at times, it was the necessary tool through which a solid foundation for us to build was created.

Enduring this has given me the strength and tenacity to bear hardship in other areas of my life such as my friendships, my career, my ministry, and my hearts desires. With all things great comes an equally as great journey that one must persevere through. The Bible says, "The race is not given to the swift nor to the strong, but to the one that endures to the end." The greatness at the end is always worth the process!

Lesson Principles:

1. A great process proceeds great purpose.

2. The journey prepares and equips you for greatness.

3. Becoming all that you were created to be is well worth all that you undergo.

Let's Pray:

Father, in the name of Jesus, Your Word declares in Ecclesiastes 9:11, "The race is not given to the swift nor the strong, but he who endures to the end." I know that You have a great plan and future in store for me. Help me to endure life's race, to the end. In Jesus' name. Amen

Lesson 31:

"Extend the Grace and Mercy You Want to Receive"

"And you know, when you've experienced grace and you feel like you've been forgiven, you're a lot more forgiving of other people. You're a lot more gracious to others." (Rick Warren)

A mirror is described as a reflective surface, accurately representing and reflecting something else. Some of us love mirrors because we are fond of the image that is reflected back to us. There are others that despise and avoid them at all cost because they are repulsed by the representation of self that is cast back. Hate it or love it, the mirror is only a messenger doing the job that it was designed to do; which is give you an accurate representation of whatever it is that you place in front of it.

Over time I've realized that God uses the people in our lives for this exact purpose. They serve as life's mirror; our reflection. With this process God is accomplishing two tasks. First, He is revealing who we really are at that time. If we pay close attention, confront the negatives and do the hard work, we have the opportunity to stretch, grow and become the best version of ourselves. On the other hand, there are times we choose to ignore certain characteristics, particularly the things that we don't like about ourselves. Because we refuse to do the work, we will continue to attract the same type of people. This catapults us into a vicious cycle that hinders our growth and delays our journey to becoming both healthy and whole.

Through this process God also teaches us the art of extending grace and mercy. These is His undeserved love and forgiveness. It is extremely difficult to love someone through their blemishes and weaknesses. Yet, this is exactly what we desire of others. We all want to be loved unconditionally and forgiven quickly. God requires us to love others with that same degree of intensity. The love and forgiveness we want to receive is the same that we are required to give. What better way to teach us this principle than to send us a mirror image of self to love, despite their flaws. We must extend grace and mercy to those who act just like we do in our most difficult and unlovable state. Here is a personal example.

My husband and I were having a rather intense disagreement. (that's my nice way of saying argument) I was usually the one whose mouth would be out of control. Unfortunately, verbal abuse was part of the baggage I brought into our marriage. This particular time, he beat me to the punch. He was yelling at the top of his lungs and saying things I'd never heard him say. I was shocked and my feelings were instantly hurt. When he finally stopped, with tears welled up in my eyes all I could say to him was, "Why would you say something like that to me?" Never once did I think of all the disrespectful or hurtful things I said to him. Nor did I take into consideration how much he had already endured. Through it all he chose to love me, unconditionally. All I could think of in the moment is how hurt I was.

I was so distraught after this argument, I suggested we see our counselor. When we got in her office the tension was so thick, I think we even scared her. By the end of our session she looked at us and shook her head. She said, "You two have literally switched rolls." I thought to myself she had to be mistaken. There's no way I ever made him feel the way he made me feel that day. Truthfully, that is exactly what I had done. I hurt my husband to his core with my words and he chose to forgive me and loved me despite it. Now it was my turn.

Not only did I need to work on changing those harmful habits, but I also needed to forgive my husband. This was not an easy task. For me the first step was acknowledging the fact that I communicate poorly when I am angry. And I couldn't just say it, I really had to own the behavior he was reflecting to me. Through my husband's actions that day, I was able to see firsthand how I spoke to and acting towards him out of anger. I could feel how it made him feel. Not only did I verbally apologize, I made up my mind to intentionally work towards change.

As difficult as this may be to imagine, you let someone down every single day, that loves you more than life itself. That someone is God. Yet, He loves us so much that He gives us brand new mercy daily. All He asks is that we love Him and love one another by extending that same grace and mercy to our fellow man. This is a difficult task under our own strength, but the Spirit of God within us empowers us makes up for all that we lack. When we look at it that way, it's not hard at all!

Lesson Principles:

1. Grace gives us what we don't deserve. Mercy protects us from what we do deserve.

2. Love people the way God loves you.

3. The Holy Spirit gives us the capacity to love unconditionally and forgive quickly.

Let's Pray:

Father God, even in our most difficult moments, especially with the most challenging people, help us to extend the same level of grace that You have extended to us. Remind us that we are imperfect beings and need Your unearned patience and love. We thank You for freely giving new grace and mercy every single day. In Jesus' name. Amen.

LESSON 32:

"Love Is All You Need"

"Love takes off masks that we fear we cannot live without and know we cannot live within." (James Baldwin)

Love is all you need. It sounds so cliché, yet it is the absolute truth. There is a power that love possesses that you cannot find in any other source in Heaven or on Earth. Love gives you the strength to stand boldly in the face of fear. It is the power that you pull from to forgive those that have wronged you and mend old wounds. It gives you the courage to be vulnerable enough to open yourself up again after being hurt. Love is the butterflies you feel in your stomach when forming a new relationship. It is also in the last tear you shed from an old one and everything in between.

Love provides a sense of determination that kicks in when you're at your wits end. It shows up when you're backed into the corners of life and need to come out fighting. It picks you up when you've been beat down. Love instills a sense of urgency when people are depending on you. It is the force that helps us to see the glass as half full.

Love saturates the heart of a person that has been deeply wounded. It is felt in the depths of a sincere apology. Love is a second chance and another and another, until the other is enough because you have finally gotten it right. Love is the capacity to forgive and the foundation for a new beginning.

The confidence of love is behind the push of the mother bird when the time comes for her chicks to fly. The gentleness is present with a lioness with her cubs. Its strength in the stride of a cheetah after his prey. The beauty of love is seen in the elongated neck and legs of the giraffe. Love's protection is in shell of a turtle. Its power is imprinted in the sharpness of a shark's teeth. And the creativity of the process from caterpillar to pupa to the emergence of a beautiful butterfly from its chrysalis; that is love.

Love is preservation and restoration. It is vindication and justification. Love is sanctification, redemption and salvation. 1 Corinthians 13:4-8 says it like this, "Love suffers long and is kind; love does not envy; love does not parade itself It is not puffed up, does not behave rudely, is not self-seeking, and is not provoked. It thinks no evil, does not rejoice in iniquity, but rejoices in the truth; bears all things, believes all things, hopes all things, endures all things. Love never fails."

Love is the very power that created this World and designed every aspect of it to run both efficiently and effectively. 1 John 4:8 proclaims that, "God is Love!" No matter how dark the day or gloomy the night; how difficult the test or tedious the trial. No matter the height of the mountain or low the valley. God is intertwined into the greatest and the worst of it all. He has been, still is and always will encompass all we will ever need!

Lesson Principles:

1. Love is the greatest source we will ever have access to.

2. Love is a necessity in every aspect of our lives, no matter how good or bad it is perceived to be.

3. God is love.

Let's Prayer:

God when we read Your description of what love is in 1 Corinthians 13:4-8, we realize what a powerful source love is for us. Help us to exude love in all that we do, say and think; first towards ourselves and then to one another. Help us remember that love is not just what You do God, love is who You are, and You never fail! In Jesus' name. Amen!

LESSON 33:

"Nothing Just Happens"

"It's the little details that are vital. Little things make big things happen." (John Wooden)

November 2008 my coworker invited me to attend church with her. The invitation took me by surprise because I didn't know she was an avid church goer. Nevertheless, she asked and I had a decision to make. I was reluctant at first for a couple reasons. One being that I hadn't stepped foot inside of a church in years. The second was my lifestyle at the time. I was afraid that I would catch fire in the vestibule before I even made it to a seat!

During that time in my life, I was living wild and reckless. My weeks consisted of sleeping until about noon, running errands, then working all afternoon. After work I'd go home just long enough to take a quick shower, get dressed, and go to the club until about 3am. I would come home and do it all over again the next day. This was my routine every week. You can probably imagine my discomfort at the thought of going to the House of God, especially since I knew better. Yet, I agreed.

Sunday had finally arrived. I remember feeling extremely nervous as I pulled into the parking lot. I sat in my car and waited for my co-worker to text me. Once I received her message, I checked my makeup in the mirror one last time, took a deep breath and headed to the door. Once I made it into the sanctuary and saw the sea of people, I felt a little better. Unlike the church I grew up in, this one was huge. I thought to myself, "There are at least a thousand people in here. I should no problem flying under the radar." I'm sure you know as well as I do we may be able to hide from man, but we are never concealed from God.

As I entered the sanctuary, I was taken aback by its beauty. The color scheme was purple and grey; it screamed royalty. There were stained-glass windows and fancy lighting everywhere. Two large monitors were placed on either side of the pulpit with a countdown to service time and inspirational music played throughout the edifice. This was not how I remembered church looking or feeling. We followed the ushers to our seats. It was rather close to the front; I believe it was the third row to be exact. The ministers sat right in front of us, dressed all in black. The musicians and choir members took their places on the stage. At exactly 11:00 simultaneously the music in the sanctuary faded and a short, dark haired woman walked up to the podium. She asked us to stand for prayer. The service began.

It all gets a little foggy from there. I remember the Spirit of the Lord moving so strongly during praise and worship that I just begin to weep uncontrollably. The pastor stepped to the microphone and begin to invite people to the altar. People were coming by the dozens, flooding the altar; I was one of them. I carried my brokenness and laid there at the altar, desperate for God. Not the God of my mother and father, but I was hungry to know God for myself. Thirsty for the inner well that I was taught would never run dry.

I realized in that moment, on that Sunday morning lying at the altar, God was everything I would ever need! That invitation to church by my co-worker seemed random at the time. It seemed like my acceptance or decline was an option. I seriously contemplated turning her down. Little did I know she was a vessel being used by God to fulfill His purpose in my life, which at the time was to draw me back to Him.

There are going to be times in your life when you're not going to know the why or how behind what's going on. You're not going to always comprehend the reason your life is going a certain way and what's more frustrating, you won't have the ability to change it. Just know that when you belong to God, NOTHING JUST HAPPENS! Every intricate detail of your life has been carefully planned out to ensure that you reach your destination, in His timing. The Bible declares in Jeremiah 1:5, "Before I formed you in the womb I knew you." God created you. He knows you. Before you were even born, He chose you for His specific purpose. Our job is to be obedient to His Word, have faith in Him, and know without the shadow of a doubt, "All things work together for good for those that love God, to them who are the called according to His purpose." (Romans 8:28)

Lesson Principles:

1. God has a specific plan and purpose for your life.

2. Everything that happens in your life pushes you closer to fulfilling your God given purpose.

3. Trust that all things work together for your good.

Let's Pray:

Lord, there are times when things happen in my life that I just don't understand. There are moments that I feel isolated and don't know how I'll make it. I pray that you will help me to know that You are in control of all aspects of my life and are always guiding my steps. I believe there is nothing that happens in my life, that You are not aware of. I thank You that everything in my life pushes me to my purpose in You. In Jesus' name. Amen.

LESSON 34:

"Much Prayer, Much Power"

"Keep on asking, and you will receive what you ask for. Keep on seeking, and you will find. Keep on knocking, and the door will be opened to you. For everyone who asks, receives. Everyone who seeks, finds. And to everyone who knocks, the door will be opened." Matthew 7:7-8

Sunday December 9th, 2007 was the day I officially made the life altering decision to dedicate the rest of my days to God. I remember like it was yesterday. I woke up that morning with my mind already made up. I had only been visiting this Church for about a month, but every time I listened to the speaker it felt as if God was talking to me specifically. Not to mention the fact that I had also met the love of my life there. I knew I had found my spiritual home.

My transformation process began almost immediately. It was an extremely noticeable change to those who knew me. I was ready to do the intense work to be better, inside and out. I went to service regularly, both Wednesday night and Sunday morning. I read my study Bible every day. I downloaded a daily devotional onto my cell phone. I listened to inspirational music and sermons on CD. I purged old friendships and intentionally tried to keep my environment as toxic free as possible. I was ready for complete mental and spiritual wholeness.

Fast forward to July 7th which is the day I married my Bobbo. We united our families and lives and started the journey to becoming one. What a tedious process it was and at times still is. I have learned the true value of building a foundation of friendship, faith, effective communication, trust, intimacy, forgiveness and love. Even when times are most challenging, we are able to make it work by getting back to the core of who we are as a couple.

Out of obedience to God and answering His call on our lives, my husband and I founded the Purpose Church. I wish I could say it was smooth sailing from there. In actuality, ALL HELL BROKE LOOSE IN OUR LIVES! We had no idea that a *yes* to God would catapult us into a season of struggle and suffering more intense than ever before. *Nothing* was off limits! Our marriage was under attack. Our children were acting out. Our exes had lost their minds. Not to mention the fact that we lost our cars and our rental property went into foreclosure. There were times during this process when we didn't even have enough money to pay our bills or buy food. On top of all that, we had to listen to family members and colleagues call us crazy for starting a ministry in the first place. All I could think was, "Seriously God?!"

The pressure of our situation began to weigh on me. I gave up the practices that gave me strength in the beginning of my Christian walk. I had gotten to the point that I didn't want to read my Bible or devotionals anymore. I wasn't praying regularly. Inspirational music made me cry and because of the drastic change in lifestyle, I lost all of my so-called friends. This was the first time in my Christian journey that I felt spiritually and emotionally depleted. More importantly, I couldn't understand where God was in all of this.

I felt like my mind was going snap; literally break under all of this pressure. It had just become too much to bear. I was ready to quit on everything; the church, the marriage, the children, life itself! I had nothing else to give. I felt as if it was them or me. Once again while in my distressed state, I was able to confide in my husband. "Shawn, you're carrying a weight that was never intended for you to carry", he said. I began to sob. He continued, "You need to give it to God. He knows the trials that we face and only He knows why. You need to lean on Him." I told him I didn't know how to release it all. Then he said something powerful that resonates with me to this day, "Shawn, prayer is one of our greatest weapons. Much prayer, much power. No prayer, no power."

It was during my most turbulent times that I so

gratefully learned the power of prayer. Philippians 4:6 says, *"Don't worry about anything; instead, pray about everything. Tell God what you need and thank Him for all He has done."* In Matthew 11:18 Jesus says, *"Come to me, all of you who are weary and carry heavy burdens, and I will give you rest.'"* Matthew 7:7-8 *says, "Keep on asking, and you will receive what you ask for. Keep on seeking, and you will find. Keep on knocking, and the door will be."* These scriptures remind us to take all of our cares, worries, burdens, and concerns to God in prayer.

Prayer is simply a conversation with God. This is where we find peace, joy and contentment, no matter what state we're in. It is through prayer that our relationship with God is developed and maintained and our faith is strengthened. When we pray, we gain the strength to endure and persevere through all circumstances and situations we must face on this journey. I will leave you with this Scripture. *"Rejoice always, pray continually, give thanks in all circumstances; for this is God's will for you in Christ Jesus."* 1 Thessalonians 5:16-18 Pray purposefully!!

Lesson Principles:

1. The more you pray, the more power you will have to stand in your situation.

2. Prayer is how we commune and build a relationship with God.

3. Always pray!

Let's Pray:

Lord help me to remember to bring all the concerns, worries, and cares that I face on this journey, to You in prayer. I thank You for the promise to give me Your unspeakable joy and peace that surpasses all understanding in return. In Jesus' name I pray. Amen.

LESSON 35:

"God's Grace is Sufficient"

2 Corinthians 12:8-9 (NLT) Three different times I begged the Lord to take it away. Each time he said, "My grace is all you need. My power works best in weakness." So now I am glad to boast about my weaknesses, so that the power of Christ can work through me.

My brother-in-law is what the average person would call an "over achiever." He graduated from high school with honors and continued to excel through college. Once he graduated from college, he didn't want just any job to make ends meet, he wanted a career with benefits and the potential for future growth. That's when his tenure with the county began.

Before the age of 30 he had already obtained a college degree, excelling in his career, was promoted twice, had two cars, a house with a picket fence, a child and two dogs! The beauty was he always attributed his success to three key components: hard work, determination, and His unwavering faith in God.

Early one Sunday morning, both favor and faith came under fire when he was involved in a horrific accident. This jovial, high spirited, hard-working, God-fearing man came face to face with an extreme personal test. This accident made him question everything he's ever believed about life and ultimately God. As I held my sister close she just kept repeating, *"I can't live without him. I just can't live without him."* My heart broke for her. I did all I could and began to talk to God within my heart. I remember saying over and over, *"God it can't end like this. You can't mean for this family to suffer like this."* I clearly heard God respond with one statement, *"My grace is sufficient."*

After several hours of surgery and countless people coming in and out of this waiting area, the doctors finally came and took my sister to a private room to give her an update on her husband's condition. When she came back, she was distraught. In that moment, the magnitude of the injuries he'd sustained was almost too much for her to bear. She yelled out to me, *"I just need you to pray. Pray NOW!"* I dropped to my knees, grabbed her hands and began to pour out my heart to God. Although I can't recall every word of this prayer, I do remember intentionally thanking God for His grace. Today my brother-in-law is not just healthy, but thriving in every area of his life! He was indeed graced for the path he has been assigned to travel. The same holds true for you.

Grace is the unmerited, undeserved, unearned, Love of God. Simply stated, grace is God's love in action. It is what strengthens and empowers us to endure and persevere through difficulties and hardships. Grace is the tool gifted to us by God which helps us complete this journey called life with victory.

For some of us, life has dealt us such extreme blows and devastating circumstances that we become fatigued. Some days it is a struggle just to get out of bed and make it through another day. God has sent me to remind you that you are still here as a testament to the power of His grace. No matter the pain, the pressure, the devastation, or heartache, know that the grace of God is enough for you to overcome any setback.

The story of Joseph in the Book of Genesis has a universal message of hope for all believers. Joseph was hated by those he loved the most for reasons beyond his control. His own brothers became so jealous that they plotted to kill him. When they couldn't go through with his murder, they decided to sell Joseph into slavery. His troubles didn't end there because Joseph had also become a target for the wife of his master. When Joseph rejected her advances, she became angry and made false allegations against him which landed him in prison.

In the face of continuous adversity, because of God's grace on his life, in the end Joseph was triumphant! Joseph never imagined that God would use the malicious intent of those around him, to propel him into his divine purpose. Before he was formed in Rachel's womb, before he was favored by his father and before his brothers tried to take his life, Joseph was already given all that he needed not just to survive the journey, but to win!

Please understand that God does not place you in a season of difficulty to destroy you. On the contrary, these burdensome moments have been tailor made for God to show His hand mightily in your life. Tribulations prepare and position you for the greatness that He has predestined for you. Life does not end in the broken place or the place of suffering. You are the child of the King! He loves you and wants the very best for you. Your destination shall be greatness! No matter what season or stage you area currently in, know that you are graced for this and His grace is enough to sustain you.

Lesson Principles:

1. Grace is the unmerited, undeserved, unearned, love of God.

2. Every believer has been gifted God's grace.

3. The grace of God is all that we need to successfully complete the process of life.

Let's Pray:

Father, in the name Jesus, although we don't pretend to understand all that we must face in the process of life. Yet, we do thank You for the grace to endure the journey and the assurance that we will come out victorious. In Jesus' name. Amen.

LESSON 36:

"Divine Connections Are Powerful"

"Divine connections are of God and are vital to your destiny and mine." (Dr. Frederick Drummond)

I received an invitation to speak at a women's conference which was themed, *"Women Empowered to Purpose"*. As I always do before I had to minister, I begin to seek God for what it was that He would have me say. What tools would He equip us with that would empower us to pursue and fulfill *His* purpose for our lives. During my prayer time Holy Spirit spoke the phrase *divine connections* to me.

A divine connection is a God ordained companionship or spiritual association created for carrying out His plan. We develop platonic relationships, business partnerships, friendships and even romantic relationships every day. Yet, most of these connections have nothing to do with the divine. If we're honest, we can admit that more times than not we neglect to consult God at all when deciding to attach ourselves to people. However, once things go left, that's when we have the audacity to cry out to God.

Oh, you know what I'm talking about. We say things like, *"Lord, why is this happening to me?" "Why is my relationship failing?" "Why did they betray our friendship?"* or *"Why is my marriage falling apart God?"* What if God's response was simply, *"Why didn't you seek me first?!"* We tend to go to God in the aftermath. In some cases it's after we have already created consequences that we're simply going to have to live with.

I believe the main reason we don't consult God first is because we don't fully understand the importance of attaching ourselves to the right people. Pastor Frederick Drummond hosted a webinar entitled *"The Importance of Divine Connections."* He opened by quoting Matthew 19:6 from the Message Bible, *"Since they are no longer two but one, let no one split apart what God has joined together."* He says, "The phrase *joined together* is derived from the Greek word "enónontai" (e'-no-no-day), which literally means to be yoked, or coupled with. In English it means association, companionship, completeness, a couple, a pair, a team."

Drummond explains that while in this context being joined together refers to marriage, in its broader application it speaks of anything or anyone that God has joined together and made *one* to further His plans and purposes. Drummond says, "No one can make it on their own. We need one another—we are social creatures and can't make it alone—we were all born to be team players. To be otherwise is to be dysfunctional."

One of the greatest Biblical examples of divine connection is the story of Naomi and Ruth. These two women endured immense tragedy, but they were bound together by a purpose greater than their pain. They lost their spouses, but gained strength from their bond with one another. Even when Naomi attempted to send Ruth away, she clung to her mother-in-law even the more. Little did they know the devastation of this loss was the gateway god would use to bless them with greater.

There are many principles we can glean from Naomi and Ruth's story that show the power of divine connections, but I chose to highlight just two.

1. Divine Connections carry a blessing for your life.
2. Divine Connections are unbreakable.

Unlike the temporary acquaintances we make with people today, God ordained relationships are created for a specific purpose and are not easily broken. They are built to take a licking and keep on ticking. Naomi pleaded with Ruth to go back to her place of stability, security and safety, her home and her gods. But there was something God had for both their lives that would only manifest through them being connected. The harder Naomi attempted to convince Ruth to leave her, the more adamant she was to stay. Something in Ruth alerted her that a greater future was attached to Naomi. Ruth didn't allow distance, culture, religion or even death to sever their bond. They were yoked together, made one by God Himself, to accomplish His perfect plan for their lives.

Pray to God to reveal *His* will and purpose for your life. Then ask Him to show you the people that He has assigned to you; to help you pursue and achieve His will. Lastly, pray that God will teach you how to nurture these relationships, so they will become all He has designed them to be.

Lesson Principles:

1. Divine Connection is God ordained.

2. Seek God for those people that He has assigned to your life.

3. They carry a blessing for your life and are unbreakable.

Let's Pray:

Lord, we thank You for creating us with a perfect plan and purpose in mind. We thank You for the people that You have assigned to our lives. We pray that every relationship that we develop be pleasing to You and that every tie outside of Your will for us be severed. In Jesus' name. Amen.

Lesson 37:

"Forgiveness: The Gift that Keeps on Giving"

"The weak can never forgive. Forgiveness is the attribute of the strong." (Mahatma Gandhi)

We've all had to battle with that big "F" word at some point in our lives. *Should I, or shouldn't I? Will I, or won't I? Why am I even thinking about this? How could they have done something like that to me?* The painful "F" word I'm referring to is, forgiveness! Then we struggle with the fact that even if we do forgive, will we ever be able to forget? We have all been guilty of harboring ill will towards others at some point or another.

I myself have fallen prey to the misfortune of being unforgiving. One of my most vivid bouts was against my own niece. I was moving and needed to sell all of the furniture in my home. I was still paying of the balance for the living room furniture. We agreed that she would take over the payments by paying me a certain amount every two-weeks, until the balance was paid in full. To make this agreement legit, I even drew up a contract for both of us to sign so we could avoid any potential discrepancies.

The very first transaction went smoothly. She met me at my place that Friday, as agreed, with cash. I gave her a receipt, deposited the money and made the payment from my account so there would be a paper trail. The next two weeks passed, but I didn't hear anything. I called and got no answer. I left messages, but received no response. I tried not to panic initially, especially since the payment wasn't due until the end of the month. However, the due date came and went, still no payment or contact. At first, I was majorly disappointed and hurt. Since there was only a two-year age difference between us, she was more like a sister to me than a niece and I expected more from her. My disappointment very quickly morphed into anger!

My unwillingness to forgive was literally controlling my emotions and feelings towards a person that had been a huge part of my support system my entire life. I didn't realize the magnitude of the effect until about two years later, while I was lying in a hospital bed. The nurse came in to tell me that I was losing my baby and would need emergency surgery. She asked if I wanted them to call anyone to come. The first person I thought of was my niece! In an instant, that one disagreement paled in comparison to the to the love and support we shared over the years. Due to my unwillingness to forgive and stubbornness, I disconnected from the one person I needed during one of my most painful moments to date.

Not once did I consider how carrying the weight of unforgiveness would affect me mentally, emotionally and even physically. From that moment, I made the conscious decision to choose to forgive. This is when the well-known cliché *"Forgiveness is a gift you give yourself"* truly became my reality. It was no longer about her and her actions or lack thereof, it was about liberating myself. Forgiveness had solely become about me living life in perfect peace and experiencing unspeakable joy. I decided to freely give love without the fear of being taken advantage of or hurt Relinquishing that burden allowed me to live a joyful and full life, as my very best self and nurture the relationships with those around me. This started with my beautiful niece. By the time we reconnected, *I* was the one apologizing to *her* for the time we lost.

Not forgiving will cost you peace, joy and love. You won't be able to embrace the beauty of life surrounding you if your head and heart are filled with hurt from your past. It is literally poison to our bodies and minds. Most times it begins with an offense that, if not dealt with, manifests into resentment and bitterness. Our hearts and minds were not created to function properly while carrying this type of negativity. Not forgiving is to drink poison while patiently waiting for the other person to die.

FREE YOURSELF! FORGIVE AND LET IT GO! Begin to live life the way it was intended. You will be grateful that you did. I'm telling you what I know!

Lesson Principles:

1. Forgiveness is a gift you give yourself!

2. Forgiving is not the same as admitting the offense didn't happen.

3. You will never live a completely liberated life, if you carry unforgiveness in your heart.

Let's Pray:

Lord, there are hurts that I carry so deeply it feels impossible to forgive. Please help me to understand the magnitude of the effect that unforgiveness has on me. Help me to embrace the benefits that the gift of forgiveness bring to every area of my life. In Jesus' name. Amen.

LESSON 38:

"Your Process Prepares You for Your Unique Purpose"

"Do not conform to expectations and limitations set by men. Only God sets the standards for you!" (LaShawn Spry)

God and I have had some rather interesting conversations over the years. One of the main questions I've asked repeatedly is *"What would You have me to do?"* I always knew He was preparing me to teach the gospel, but I wondered who would listen to me. Sometimes you look at the people that are doing the very thing that your heart desires and you can't help but commit that ultimate faux pas. You begin to compare yourself to them. That's exactly what I started to do.

Ministering to women is my life's passion. God has given me the gift of encouraging, inspiring and empowering women to be spiritually, emotionally and mentally healed and whole. I am sure this is one thing that brings God complete glory in my life. However in my mind, I struggled with the thought that the woman already doing what I've been called to do, don't look like me. She doesn't have a messy back story like me. This woman has seemingly always had a personal relationship with God. Unlike me, she's gone to seminary and served faithfully in ministry. She's only been married once and they are raising their children under one roof. She developed a well calculated plan and followed it. Now she's living her dream; seemingly *my* dream.

This is not my story. I was nothing like the woman in my head, that I constantly compared myself to. I didn't follow the straight and narrow path, nor did I do everything right. I wasn't the woman that learned from others' mistakes in hopes of never following in their footsteps. On the contrary, I learned everything the hard way. I consistently made mistakes. Instead of college, I chose a marriage that failed miserably. I had tattoo and body piercings; went to clubs and drank alcohol. For a long time turmoil, pain and other consequences of my reckless living permeated my life. *This* was my story. A story of that filled me with guilt and shame. A way of life that distanced me from God.

One day God revealed the beauty in my distinct story. He said, *"Your journey is a picture of my grace and mercy. It is the epitome of repentance and redemption, victory and triumph. You are the sheep that was once lost; the 1 I left the 99 to find. You were blinded by sin, but now can see clearly. Your brokenness has been healed and your mind renewed. You are now fully capable of being the vessel that I always intended for you to be. Go and point others back to me."*

My purpose is to minister this truth to women like me. I am not called to the perfect, but the purposed. My testimony is for the hurting and the broken; those weighed down by guilt and shame. Women that have made mistake after mistake, bad decision after bad decision. Those who feel that they have strayed too far away and cannot find their way back. My story is specifically for you. My unique process prepared me to speak effectively into your life, just as yours is preparing you for others.

Before doubt tempts you to tune me out, let me share with you a few important nuggets that I needed to learn:

1) God loves you and there is no mistake you will make that will ever change that.

2) God is knocking at the door of your heart; waiting patiently to heal *every* hurt and carry *every* burden you bare.

3) Your process is strategically designed to prepare you for purpose.

I don't know who I'm writing this for, but you know who you are. If this has pierced your heart, God is talking directly to you. He is calling you imperfect woman, to do a perfect work for Him. Please don't ignore Him. Have your own personal conversation with Him. God is always listening.

It is your time! Time for the purposeful women to stand up confident and liberated. Take your rightful place in the Earth as Kingdom representatives. No longer highlighting your imperfections, but being a light for and bringing glory to our perfect God!

Lesson Principles:

1. Never compare your process to others.

2. Your unique process prepares you for your individual purpose.

3. Trust that God is in control of the journey and leading you exactly where you need to go.

Let's Pray:

God, Your word declares the steps of a good man are ordered by You. Continue to order my steps and help me to know that You are leading me to the exact place that You have called me to. In Jesus' name. Amen.

LESSON 39:

"The Gift of Gratitude"

"Here's the gift of gratitude: In order to feel it, your ego has to take a backseat. What shows up in its place is greater compassion and understanding. Instead of being frustrated, you choose appreciation. And the more grateful you become, the more you have to be grateful for." Oprah Winfrey

Thanksgiving is my absolute favorite holiday. As a little girl I would stay up all night with my mommy as she prepared the house to receive our entire family. She would begin the preparation process early that week. We cleaned the house from corner to corner, no stone left unturned. She would stand over the stove for hours at a time, filling every pot and pan with different food items, multiple seasonings and a whole lot of love. My favorite part of the cooking was me licking the cake bowl and mixing spoon clean! By Thursday morning the scent of oxtails, ham, collard greens, macaroni and cheese, dressing, candied yams, cornbread, sweet potato pies and pound cake filled the air.

These are some of my fondest memories. Yet, this isn't the only reason Thanksgiving is my holiday of choice. My enchantment with this holiday is nestled tightly within the spirit of gratitude. Gratitude is defined as the quality of feeling or being thankful. It is the state of being grateful; a readiness to show appreciation. Each year around this time, the atmosphere is charged with an overwhelming sense of thankfulness; people simply being grateful. It's not that our concerns and/or issues magically disappear, but instead of harboring on them we tend to focus on the good in everything and everyone.

As I got older I began to comprehend the fact that gratitude is a choice. It doesn't have to be just one day a year, but a choice we can make every single day, for the rest of our lives. It is the conscious decision to be thankful, no matter what. When we aren't diligent in our pursuit of gratitude, we run the risk of falling into the trap of its great adversaries. I love the way Ruth Neubauer, writer for the *Huffington Post*, describes it. She says,

> *"The opposite of gratitude is self-absorption which comes in many forms: guilt, entitlement, manipulating others, never being able to say you're sorry, inability to let go of anger, rumination, fears, and anxiety. 'About me' removes the ability to be grateful."*

Gratitude is a gift that requires a heart that is ready to receive and a mind clear of negativity. It is a present that once opened, releases unlimited power into all areas of our lives. It transforms dissatisfaction with our lives into contentment in whatever state we are in. Being grateful repositions our thinking from lack to more abundant living and reminds us that we are victorious in whatever circumstance we find ourselves. Even in the face of life's most challenging moments, gratitude evokes a spirit of joy and gladness that enables us to not only endure, but persevere.

The Bible itself speaks volumes of the benefits of gratitude.

"Don't worry about anything; instead, pray about everything. Tell God what you need and thank him for all he has done. Then you will experience God's peace, which exceeds anything we can understand. His peace will guard your hearts and minds as you live in Christ Jesus."

Philippians 4:6-7 (KJV)

"Be thankful in all circumstances, for this is God's will for you who belong to Christ Jesus."

1 Thessalonians 5:18 (KJV)

"Devote yourselves to prayer with an alert mind and a thankful heart."

Colossians 4:2 (KJV)

"And give thanks for everything to God the Father in the name of our Lord Jesus Christ."

Ephesians 5:20 (KJV)

Gratitude is a gift from God. It is an ability freely given to His children to live a life free of anxiety, discontent, depression, and worry. We have the liberty to dance, sing, praise, and worship despite our current circumstances because we know who is *truly* in control. In the words of gospel recording artist Travis Greene, *"All things are working for my good. He's intentional, never failing!"* And that purposeful people, is reason in itself to be grateful.

Lesson Principles:

1. Gratitude is a gift we choose to unwrap every day.

2. Gratitude releases power to endure and persevere through whatever you're facing.

3. Negativity and gratitude cannot operate in the same mental space.

Let's Pray:

God, we thank You for the gift of gratitude. Thank You for the accessibility to a life with a mindset of more than enough and a heart filled with thankfulness and joy. Help us remember that gratitude is the key that unlocks the door to more. In Jesus' name we pray. Amen.

LESSON 40:

"Take God at His Word"

"God is not a man, so he does not lie. He is not human, so he does not change his mind." (Numbers 23:19a)

The beautiful thing about learning lessons is that you will be presented with the opportunity to apply all that you have learned. As I sit here writing this chapter I am smack dab in the middle of one of these opportunities. My ability to stand on God's promises is currently being tested. Not in just one area, but in several different areas in my life simultaneously. But I cannot ignore all that I have already learned about God and the strength we gain when we hold on to His word!

I can recall reading the story of the children of Israel when as a newly converted Christian. I was frustrated by their mistrust in God. I would speak out loud to the Scriptures, *"This is the same God that just parted the Red Sea for you and you're complaining about being in the wilderness with no food? SERIOUSLY?! You're only alive right now because of Him!"* I professed to God in prayer how much I trust Him and how I would never be like that. I wouldn't thank Him for the miracle in one breath and then turn around and doubt Him with the next. Little did I know, that declaration would be tested.

The favor of God has been on the union between me and Bobby since we started dating. He showed my husband

and I that we have great purpose together and if we keep Him first, He would prosper us. In July 2017, we celebrated nine years of marriage and six years in ministry. By then we had overcome so many different challenges and obstacles. Within our first month of marriage we had one of our most tumultuous arguments to date. Two months later we moved into a condominium that was in a neighborhood straight from hell. We literally called it the projects. Four years after moving in and one month after planting the church, we were served foreclosure papers. We found out the landlord was taking our money and not paying the mortgage. Three months after that, with only six payments left, one of our two cars was repossessed. A week later, the engine in the other died. That's not even including the woes that came from us being a blended family.

We were mentally tired and spiritually drained. Regardless of how we felt, if we were going to win in life together, we knew we had to take God at His Word. God promised there was greatness and purpose attached to this marriage. No matter what our reality said, we had to learn to stand unwaveringly on His Word. Through the tears, confusion, and desire for the difficult times to end, we had to trust God. I found that we were not unlike my brothers and sisters, the children of Israel. There were times that we would grumble and complain and tell God we were better off *before* He stepped in. Yet just as patient, loving, and faithful as He was with them, so He was with us.

Now as I sit here in the middle of my bed reflecting on our season of difficulties, I do so with a heart of gratitude. Grateful that God never changed His mind about us or went back on His word. Grateful that life pushed us to pray and those prayers strengthened our relationship with God. Grateful that God taught us the power of our faith. Grateful that we now know firsthand that He is a protector, provider, miracle worker, a healer, and a keeper of His word. I am ultimately grateful that our valley experiences taught us to take God at His word!

We as believers have been given the responsibility of standing on the promises of God, in the face of opposition and adversity. Although at times it is an arduous task, we are equip with the necessary tools that enable us to do it. Faith, prayer, hope and love empowers us with the strength to hold on to God's promises, until we see them manifest. Then we are able to use our experiences to encourage others.

Allow the difficulties of life to push you closer to God and strengthen your faith in Him. When your heart is heavy, talk to Him in prayer. Study the Word of God. Learn the promises He has ordained for your life and speak them out loud. Have faith and let patience work it's perfect work within you. Most importantly, take God at His word. If He spoke it, it *shall* come to pass!

Lesson Principles:

1. If God said it, it will happen!

2. Allow the process of life to build your trust in God.

3. God does not want to break you; on the contrary His intent is to build you.

Let's Pray:

Father, in the name of Jesus, I thank You for Your promises being yes and amen. I choose to trust You and take You at Your word, no matter what. In Jesus' name. Amen.

ACKNOWLEDGMENTS

To the One that created me, forgave me, saved me, cleansed me, renewed me, graced me, and purposed me. God everything I do is out of obedience to, faith in and love for You.

To my heart and soul, Red and Tre. Mommy covers you in prayer every single day and will carry you in my heart until I take my last breath.

To my Harlem Lotus, you are the sunshine of my life!

To my Fly Spry guy. Your feet pursued me. Your words wooed me. Your ears heard me. Your mind thought of me. Your arms held me. Your heart carried me. Your prayers covered me. Your love healed me. Without you, my life just doesn't flow the same. In the words of India Arie, *"If I am a reflection of him, then I must be FLY."* #SpryChronicles

ABOUT THE AUTHOR

LaShawn Spry, affectionately known as *Your Purpose Pusher* is a pastor, psalmist, author, certified life coach, calculated planner, motivational speaker, and talk show host. She has been gifted with the ability to utilize her wisdom, knowledge, life experiences and spiritual gifts to ignite purpose in women.

LaShawn began her career with the Police Department in 1998. Very quickly a spark ignited within her; a desire to help people. Years later she began serving at the Antioch Missionary Baptist Church of Miami Gardens, under the pastoral leadership of Pastor Arthur Jackson III. This is where she met her husband, Pastor Robert E. Spry II.

After receiving the call of God upon her life, she was ordained as an Evangelist in June 2011. In November of that same year, she and her husband founded the Purpose Church in Miami Gardens, FL. Their mission is to cultivate potential and propel people to purpose through ministry.

In June 2017, LaShawn was ordained as a Pastor and now serves as Associate Pastor, alongside her husband.

LaShawn has a passion for motivating and encouraging women. She assists them with fulfilling their God-given purpose. Because of this, she enrolled in the Bentley Coaching Institute January 2012, where she obtained her Life Coaching Certification. She then founded "Purposeful Living with LaShawn Spry", where her mission is to utilize her life experiences and spiritual gifts to encourage, inspire and empower the purpose-driven woman to be successful in every area of her life. LaShawn specializes in one-on-one coaching and motivational speeches which challenge women to cultivate their God-given potential. She also developed a calculated plan that has the power to transfer your visions and dreams from your heart to your hands. Lastly, LaShawn has established a mentoring group called "Forever Becoming" to assist in the development of powerful girls and young women. The mentoring group allows members to discover and live their purpose.

LaShawn is pursuing a Bachelor of Science in Psychology at Liberty University. She and her husband are a blended family and are the proud parents of three handsome sons and four beautiful daughters.

LaShawn Spry|Your Purpose Pusher
"Vibe with me, I'll change your life!"

www.ingramcontent.com/pod-product-compliance
Lightning Source LLC
LaVergne TN
LVHW051826080426
835512LV00018B/2746